Whitewater Handbook
3d edition

Bruce Lessels

APPALACHIAN MOUNTAIN CLUB BOOKS
BOSTON, MASSACHUSETTS

Cover photo: Scott Underhill
Cover and book design: Carol Bast Tyler
Illustrations: John Urban, Noland Hisey, and David Eden

Distributed by The Talman Company.

Library of Congress Cataloging-in-Publication Data
Lessels, Bruce.
    Whitewater handbook / Bruce Lessels. — 3rd ed.
        p. cm.
    Includes bibliographical references (p. 261) and index.
    ISBN 1-878239-01-5 : $14.95
    1. Whitewater canoeing—Handbooks, manuals, etc. I. Title.
GV788.L47   1991
797.1'22—dc 20   93-21066
                                                                       CIP

The paper used in this publication meets the minimum requirements of the American National Standard for Information Sciences—Permanence of Paper for Printed Library Materials, ANSI Z39.48–1984.∞

**Due to changes in conditions,
use of the information in this book
is at the sole risk of the user.**

Printed on recycled paper with soy-based inks.

Printed in the United States of America.

10 9 8 7 6 5 4 3 2 1   94 95 96 97 99

Contents

*To my wife
and my mother,
who have supported my paddling career
financially, emotionally, and with endless amounts
of time and energy.*

Acknowledgments

This is the third edition of an instruction manual about what was an obscure pastime and is now a growing sport. I owe the largest debt of gratitude to the first two writers: John Urban and T. Walley Williams III. Urban's original book captured the rhythm and feel of whitewater in a way that, upon reading it twenty-eight years later, makes me realize the sport has only changed outwardly since he wrote. The soul of the sport is still the same. I have used parts of his introduction as this book's introduction with some editing to reflect recent changes in the sport.

T. Walley's revision, written in 1981, preserved as much of Urban's original as possible, while adding chapters that updated techniques and equipment. His contribution was technical, clarifying what was unclear in the first edition and adding or modifying material where techniques had changed. My debt to T. Walley, however, goes far beyond the book. He introduced me to the sport of whitewater. Without T. Walley's support and encouragement as I was learning about strokes, braces, eddy turns, and peelouts, I would not be writing this book today.

Jamie McEwan, Doug Gordon, Charlie Walbridge, and Joan and Bill Hildreth read drafts of the manuscript and helped bring my technique descriptions in line with the state of the art. To Jamie and his wife, Sandy, I am especially indebted—I count myself lucky to be among the paddlers they have inspired through their great love for the sport and their generous support. Gordon Hardy at the AMC initiated this project and, as editor, has been instrumental in helping me carry it out. Bill and Joan Hildreth, Tom Christopher, Shirley Griffith, Karen Blom, Peter Franzoso, Noland Hisey, Sanne van der Ros, Jim Dowd, Jon Goodman, Earl Alderson, Linda Kazimierczyk, Susan Connolly, Jim Gariepy, Jobeth Hager, David Hearn, Andy Bridge, Jeff DeFeo Inner Mountain Photography, Landis Arnold, Robert Harrison, Slim Ray, and Bob Foote appeared in and helped me shoot the photos that accompany the text. Noland Hisey and David Eden provided the illustrations. David Rose of Dagger Canoes supplied technical information about roto–molded and blow–molded kayaks.

Preface

This is a guide to a sport that has taken me from New Hampshire to Chile. It has taught me the value of persistence, the importance of hard work, and the joy of self-expression. I have tried to write a complete overview of the sport for the beginner, introduce a variety of advanced techniques for the intermediate, and point out technical subtleties for the expert. But there are inherent limitations to any instruction book that must be stated up front. Nothing can substitute for expert instruction, since the real learning in any sport comes in the school of hard knocks.

No matter what level paddler you are, keep in mind that the best paddlers are also the most innovative and are constantly reassessing their technique. Most paddlers are out on the river to do their own thing, so being told they're doing the wrong thing, or that what they're doing isn't as worthwhile as what someone else is doing, is stifling. Of course in a whitewater handbook, some judgments of good and bad technique are essential. I have tried, however, to present different approaches where appropriate, with the knowledge that in an evolving sport any instruction book is likely to become obsolete eventually. I encourage each reader to try variations of these techniques as he or she sees fit, always keeping an open mind and remembering that each of us is in the sport to paddle our own canoe or kayak; no one likes a back-seat driver.

Safety and liability are inescapable issues in paddlesport. Whitewater has inherent risks, but it is largely these risks that draw people to it. Each person must decide for him- or herself what level of personal risk feels right and when his or her own actions put someone else at risk. For instance, while the general rule for running rivers is that you should always have at least three boaters for safety, there are plenty of excellent paddlers who routinely run rivers in groups of two, and even a few who occasionally run rivers alone. It boils down to judgment. The rules of safety given in this book are to be viewed as general guidelines. As a beginner you should follow them word for word. However, as you develop experience and judgment in river situations, you may adapt these rules to fit a particular circumstance. In every situation, there are two questions you should ask yourself: "Am I willing to accept this risk?" and "Am I putting other people at risk beyond what they are prepared to accept?"

There are subtleties to paddling that take years to learn and vary from individual to individual. Some are best communicated through photographs or drawings, so I have tried to illustrate each technique that is not easily explained in words. Yet even photographs cannot convey the feelings or the rhythms of river running. In the end, nothing can teach you to paddle like a river.

Introduction

What is whitewater? It is a light boat in a fast rapid, a game of skill played against a river, a sport in which wit and subtlety outrank muscle. It is the passage of a wilderness stream, a weekend's paddling for its own sake, and the few intense minutes of effort and precision of a slalom race. The constant elements are skill in handling the boat and a close knowledge of the ways of moving water.

The modern canoe comes in a direct line from North American Indians, who used their boats much as we do, if for more practical reasons. Like ours, their canoes were designed to carry wilderness duffel, to survive rough stretches of open water, or to run difficult rapids, and the various shapes they evolved were remarkably like those we use today. The most striking innovation, dating back only to the 1950s is the closed canoe, also known as a C-1 or C-2, with a completely enclosed hull, like a kayak. Since it is intended for whitewater sport alone, it may be small in all dimensions and provide no more than minimum room for gear.

Open canoes have also evolved. They are now easier to turn and drier than they were ten years ago. With recent advances in outfitting and skills, open and closed canoeists are able to keep up with, and often surpass, kayakers on difficult river runs and first descents.

The kayak comes to us from the Eskimos by way of Europe, where it was adapted from the original slim hunting craft first for comfortable river touring and, more recently, for whitewater paddling. Touring kayaks, more similar to the original Eskimo boats in design but built of more durable modern materials, have made a dramatic comeback in recent years, yet they are awkward in rapids, where agility and responsiveness are primary requirements. The evolution of the design of the whitewater kayak within the last thirty years has produced superb boats for playing waves, holes, and eddies; jumping off waterfalls; or racing down difficult whitewater.

The sport of whitewater offers opportunities to suit different temperaments, athletic abilities, and personalities. Wilderness tripping uses whitewater skills to explore remote regions accessible only by rapid-flowing rivers. Some of today's wilderness trippers are pushing the limits of the sport by running class V rivers many days away from civilization. Recreational whitewater paddling, or cruising, is a great way to escape for a few hours to several days, running relatively accessible, but often difficult, rivers. Recreational paddlers "play" the river, using its power to perform acrobatic maneuvers such as enders, or hopping into and out of eddies, turning the river into a natural slalom course. Two more recent offshoots of recreational paddling are whitewater rodeos, where paddlers compete to see who can put on the most acrobatic performance, and steep creeking, where paddlers run very narrow rivers with high gradients.

Whitewater racing takes place on moderately difficult rapids and involves either a point-to-point wildwater race or a shorter, but more technically demanding, slalom race. Racers have often led recreational paddlers in technique, since good technique can mean several seconds' difference on a race course.

Squirt boating is a recent phenomenon and has had a tremendous impact on every aspect of the sport, from the equipment to the lingo. Using very small, flat boats, squirt boaters perform tricks and maneuvers that paddlers would never have dreamed of fifteen years ago.

Whether you decide to pursue squirting, wilderness tripping, racing, or playboating, you'll need a solid foundation in basic techniques. The first section of this book, "The Basics," is designed to lay this foundation. The second section, "Advanced Techniques," builds on the first by offering an overview of more specialized areas of the sport.

Section I

The Basics

There's so much to learn about all at once in whitewater. Before getting into the boat and on the water, let's review some equipment and terms (these will be covered in more detail later, but for now here is an introduction). Then we'll go on to the essentials of strokes, leans, braces, river reading, rolling, safety, and more.

Chapter One

First Steps

EQUIPMENT BASICS

The three primary types of boats used on whitewater are canoes, kayaks, and inflatables (rafts and inflatable kayaks). This book covers canoes and kayaks. Several other excellent books cover inflatable technique.

Closed boats—boats with decks to keep the water out—include kayaks and closed canoes (C-1s and C-2s). Kayaks are decked boats between nine and fifteen feet long (fig. 1). They have small oval cockpit openings that are covered by neoprene or nylon sprayskirts to keep the water out. Kayakers sit almost on the bottoms of their boats with their legs straight out in front of them. They use double-bladed paddles.

Closed canoes, or C-1s and C-2s, are also decked boats and to the uninitiated look very similar to kayaks, although they are

Fig. 1. *A typical whitewater kayak at play.* Bruce Lessels

Fig. 2. *A closed canoe, or C-1.* Jobeth Hager

slightly wider and vary in length from ten to fifteen feet (fig. 2). They have more or less round cockpit openings. C-1s are one-person, or solo, closed canoes. C-2s are two-person, or tandem, closed canoes. The one or two cockpit openings are also water-proofed by sprayskirts. C-1ers and C-2ers kneel in their boats and use single-bladed canoe paddles.

Open boats are what we recognize as traditional canoes, although most open boats designed for whitewater are special-ized, departing in both form and function from traditional designs. Open canoes come in one-person models, or OC-1s (fig. 3), and two-person models, or OC-2s (fig. 4); they range in length between eleven and sixteen feet. Both are usually filled with flotation material such as air bags or foam, which displaces water, making them easier to rescue in the event of a capsize. Canoe paddlers kneel and use single-bladed paddles.

Which boat should you paddle—a canoe or a kayak? For some people the decision is simple; if you have a bum knee, you may not be able to stand the kneeling position used in canoeing; a bad back may prevent you from kayaking, since the sitting position, with legs straight out in front, can exacerbate lower-back problems. For most people, however, the choice is a matter of personal preference. If you start out in a kayak, you may

Fig. 3. *A solo open canoe, or OC-1.* Bruce Lessels

Fig. 4. *A tandem open canoe, or OC-2.* Bruce Lessels

become a kayaker simply because that boat is available. Many canoeists enjoy the challenge of using only one blade, and an equal number of kayakers see no reason to burden themselves with an off side, preferring to paddle with a blade on both sides. Some open canoers find C-1s, C-2s, and kayaks too claustrophobic. They prefer a boat that is as easy to exit from as possible if they were to get pinned against an obstruction. The extra volume in an open boat also makes it better for long trips where space for storing gear is vital. Social concerns enter into the decision for many paddlers who prefer to paddle tandem in a closed or open canoe; they may want to paddle with a husband or wife, or use canoeing as a way to meet new friends. Of course you don't have to make a decision at all. There are some paddlers who cross over, paddling canoe and kayak equally well and enjoying each boat for its specific advantages and idiosyncracies.

TERMINOLOGY BASICS

The language of whitewater paddling is as colorful as the sport itself. From "eddy turns" to "boofs," "duffeks" to "mystery moves," the terminology is at times technically descriptive, while at other times it is eccentric. This section roughly defines some basic terms that are used in the following descriptions of technique. Many of these terms are more completely defined later in the book.

A *boater*, or *paddler*, refers to either a kayaker or a canoeist. An *eddy* is an area of calm water behind (i.e., downstream of) a rock or other obstacle (fig. 5). Eddies are often used as stopping places in the middle of rapids. A *hole*, or *hydraulic*, forms when water falling over a ledge or other submerged obstacle moves back upstream below the drop forming a white, frothy recirculating current (fig. 6).

The basic whitewater moves are the *eddy turn*, *peelout*, and *ferry*. An eddy turn allows a boater to enter an eddy in order to rest or reconnoiter the rapids below. A boater sitting in an eddy uses a peelout to reenter the current and proceed downstream. Ferrying is a method of crossing from one side of the river to the other without being drawn downstream by the current.

Fig. 5. *An eddy behind a midstream boulder.* Bruce Lessels

Fig. 6. *A typical hole on a ledgy river. Note that the recycle angles downhill as it feeds back into the hole.* Karen Blom

GETTING INTO THE BOAT

Flipping while getting into your boat is a wet, embarrassing way to begin a river run. With a little care, you can be sure of a dry beginning. Whitewater boaters generally enter (or "put onto") rivers in eddies, with their boats pointing upstream. This allows them to enter the current with maximum control.

Canoe

To get into a tandem canoe, have one partner steady the boat while the other partner holds onto both gunwales, steps one foot into the middle of the boat, and kneels down into her seat. Once the first partner is in, she should hold the boat into shore with her paddle or hand while the other paddler enters in the same fashion (fig. 7).

Getting into a solo canoe can be a bit more difficult, since there is no partner to hold the boat. A solo canoe paddler should follow the same procedure as tandem paddlers, except

Fig. 7. *The bow paddler is holding the canoe into shore while her partner steps into the stern.* Bruce Lessels

he must quickly make the transition from having one foot on shore and the other in the middle of the boat to placing both feet into the boat and kneeling down.

Closed canoes present additional difficulties, since they are generally tippier and may take on water in turbulent eddies until the sprayskirt is attached. The entrance technique is the same as for tandem or solo open canoes (with the front deck substituting for the gunwales as a point of stability), but the paddler needs to balance very carefully on the way in and must attach the sprayskirt as quickly as possible to avoid taking on water.

Kayak

It's easier to enter a kayak if you use the paddle as an outrigger between the boat and shore. Place the paddle with one blade on shore and the shaft over the rear deck just behind the cockpit rim. Facing the front of the boat, grasp the paddle shaft and the back of the rim in the hand closest to the water. Place the other hand on the paddle shaft between the boat and shore. Now, keeping your weight primarily over the hand at the back of the cockpit rim, and slightly toward the shore, step into the cockpit with both feet, one at a time, and sit down into the boat (fig. 8).

Fig. 8. *Using the paddle for support while getting into a kayak.* Noland Hisey

This technique may not be appropriate if you have a new or especially delicate paddle, since it places an unusual amount of stress on the shaft. An alternate method is simply to balance carefully with one hand on the stern deck and the other on shore until your legs are safely inside the boat and you're sitting down.

Once in the boat, bring your paddle around to the front, then attach your sprayskirt. Starting in the back, work with both hands simultaneously toward the front of the rim, making sure the skirt is tucked under the coaming (the raised rim around the cockpit) all the way around (fig. 9). Always check the loop of shock cord or webbing at the front of your sprayskirt, known as the grab loop, to be sure it is outside the boat, where it can be reached quickly in the event you capsize and need to exit underwater.

Fig. 9. *Attaching a sprayskirt in a closed boat. Start in the back and work toward the front of the rim.* Bruce Lessels

WET EXITS

For maximum control on whitewater you should fit snugly in your boat, but you must also be sure you can get out of it easily if you capsize. You hold yourself in the boat with muscle power, so a supertight fit is not necessary. Your choice of fit should be based on your ability, always keeping in mind that a tighter fit also means a greater potential for serious entrapment. Beginning kayakers and closed canoeists should practice wet exits early on, and all paddlers should practice wet exits when they get a boat with different outfitting or a new design.

To wet exit from a kayak or a canoe, tuck forward and "kiss the deck" as you flip over (fig. 10). This position protects your face and torso from rocks you might encounter underwater and releases you from your outfitting. Next, let go of your paddle with one hand and pull the grab loop with the other, releasing the skirt. Now put both hands on the boat next to your hips and

Fig. 10. *Tucking forward on the way over will protect your face and torso.* Bruce Lessels

push out as if you were taking off a pair of pants (you are still holding the paddle with one hand). Think about somersaulting forward as your legs leave the boat in order to keep your body in a protected position.

Once you are out of the boat and have surfaced next to it, reach the nearest grab loop with the hand in which you are still holding your paddle. Use the other hand to swim to shore or to hold onto a rescuer's boat. If holding onto your equipment jeopardizes your safety, let go and concentrate your efforts on self-rescue.

Chapter Two

Beginning Strokes

Most of the important work in canoeing or kayaking involves an interaction of the paddle with the water. For learning purposes it is convenient to organize these interactions into strokes. However, keep in mind that an experienced boater uses his paddle in many ways. After mastering the standard strokes, variations and in-between strokes will come to mind naturally as you continue the process of mastering your environment.

Using the entire upper body to transmit power is essential to good stroke technique. The larger muscles of the torso are considerably more powerful than the arm muscles and can deliver more force over longer periods of time without tiring. It helps to keep a few basic concepts in mind:

- A straight arm is the most efficient means to transmit the pull generated by torso rotation to the paddle. This allows you to pull through the bones and tendons rather than the arm muscles, which would otherwise have to be used to maintain a bent arm.

- All strokes should happen in front of your body. Instructors at the Nantahala Outdoor Center have come up with a concept to help teach this in which you imagine a box in front of your torso. The box is defined by the outsides of your shoulders, the top of your head, and the horizontal plane at the level of the deck in front of you (fig. 11). All strokes happen with your arms in this box. If a stroke requires you to place your paddle out to the side of the boat, for instance, rotate your torso to that side in order to move the box and keep your arms within it.

- The upper and lower body should act independently of each other. This allows the upper body to be involved in a

Fig. 11. *Keeping your arms within an imaginary box in front of your body plane helps bring your torso muscles into play on all strokes.* Noland Hisey

draw stroke on the right side, while the lower body is lean-ing the boat to the left. This is especially important in low-volume boats and is easier for people with greater torso flexibility.

- Finally, canoe/kayak strokes are usually thought of as methods of moving the paddle through the water in order to make the boat move. It is more useful, however, to think of strokes as causing the boat to move around a stationary paddle. This encourages you to place your paddle in the water so it "sticks," gaining the maximum possible pur-chase, while the boat is made to move toward or around the paddle. Kayakers often think of using their legs, feet, and torso to pull the boat toward their paddles, and canoeists can use their knees, thighs, and stomach muscles to pull their boats toward their paddles.

Where you place your hands on the paddle is determined by several factors. A standard kayak hand position places the hands about four inches from the throat of the paddle. A stan-dard canoe hand position places the bottom hand either above or below the gunwale in an open canoe and just slightly above the deck in a closed canoe. This usually results in the bottom hand being four to six inches above the throat of the paddle. In both boats, don't be afraid to choke up on the paddle at times, since the extra leverage gained often results in a more powerful and effective stroke. A useful drill to practice choking up on your paddle is to paddle forward on flatwater, varying your grip from low to high on every other stroke. In a kayak, practice sliding one hand up for awhile, then practice with the other. The idea is to develop a feel for how much you are choking up, so that you can do it quickly and accurately when needed.

A few standard terms are useful when describing paddle strokes. The phases of a stroke are called the *catch, power phase ,* and *recovery.* The catch is when you initially place the paddle in the water. The power phase is the working part of the stroke, where the paddle is moving through the water and propelling or turning the boat. The recovery begins at the end of the power phase, as the paddle is being returned to the catch, where it will begin another stroke. The recovery may happen out of the water, by lifting the blade slightly and moving it back to the catch, or in the water, by feathering the blade (slicing it through the water at an angle that provides the least resistance) back to the catch.

Paddles have three primary parts: shaft, blade, and grip (figs. 12 and 13). The grip is usually a t grip on a whitewater canoe paddle. On a kayak paddle, the grip is the portion of the shaft where the paddler normally holds his hands (fig. 13). The throat is the intersection of the blade and the shaft. The power face of the blade is that face that transmits the force of the stroke to the water; i.e., the power face on a canoe or kayak forward stroke is the one facing toward the rear of the boat.

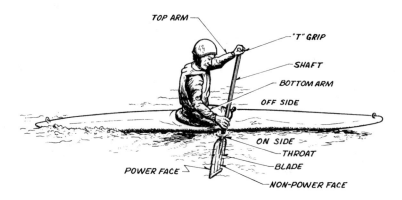

Fig. 12. *Anatomy of a canoeist and canoe paddle.* Noland Hisey

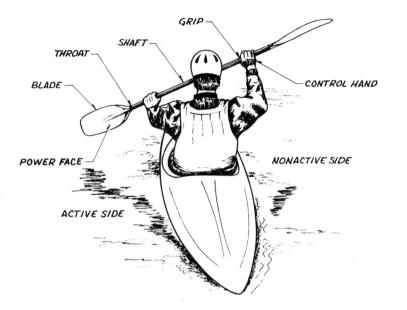

Fig. 13. *Anatomy of a kayaker and kayak paddle.* Noland Hisey

The control hand is the hand that determines the angle of the blade. For kayakers, this is the hand that remains stationary on the paddle shaft (fig. 13), while canoeists' control hands are their top, or t grip, hands (fig. 12). The bottom arm and hand are those closest to the paddle blade that is in the water. The top arm and hand are those farther away from the paddle blade that is in the water. For kayakers this varies, but for canoeists, the top hand/arm is always the t grip hand/arm, and the bottom is always the shaft hand/arm.

A canoeist's on side is the side on which he is paddling in a regular forward stroke. His off side is the side on which, to take a stroke, he must cross his blade over the boat. A kayaker's active blade is the one that is in the water during a particular stroke. The active side is the side of the boat on which the active blade is working. This terminology can also be used to refer to one side's arm, hand, and shoulder in a kayak.

STROKES FOR THE CANOE (C-1, OC-1, OC-2)

Stroke techniques for tandem and solo canoeing share far more similarities than differences. Tandem canoeists enjoy a division of labor between the bow and the stern, with one often acting as the steering wheel while the other acts as the engine. Solo canoeists, on the other hand, must both steer and propel the boat from one position. The strokes presented below are all used at certain times in both solo and tandem paddling. Some, like cross strokes, are seldom (if ever) used in the stern of a tandem boat but are equally important in the bow of a tandem boat or in a solo boat. Others, such as the forward or reverse sweep, are used in their entirety in a solo boat but adapted for tandem paddling by cutting off the beginning or the end depending on the paddler's position in the boat. In this section any particular adaptation for solo or tandem paddling is described under the description of each technique.

Canoe forward stroke

An efficient forward stroke takes hundreds of miles of paddling and careful observation to develop. This technique is the basis for good form on all other strokes, so it's worth spending the time to perfect it. Practice forward paddling on flatwater, where the distractions of whitewater are absent and you can concentrate on one aspect of technique at a time.

Forward strokes run the gamut from those that use predominantly arm muscles to those that incorporate the larger torso muscles. You should be able to do both types, since different situations call for different techniques. On difficult whitewater moves, arm paddling is often necessary, since there are so many things going on at once that to add torso twist is beyond anyone's abilities. Paddling at a higher stroke rate is also easier using more arm than torso. Cruising in between rapids, you may revert to a longer stroke where you rest by pausing momentarily during the correction at the end.

The stroke described here is a classic stroke using the entire torso, since this is technically the most difficult to do. Many of its principles apply to the other variations.

Forward paddling can be broken down in many different ways, but for the purpose of isolating the mechanics and biomechanics involved, it is here broken into three elements: torso twist (the engine), arm position (the drive shaft), and corrections (the steering wheel). While this description will treat only one element at a time, remember that it's the smooth combination of all three elements that makes a good stroke.

Torso twist. Sitting with your boat flat on the water, rotate your torso about your spine and bring your shoulders in line with the long axis of the boat. Point your on-side shoulder toward the bow (fig. 14). Your chest and shoulders should face toward your off side. Now unwind your torso until your shoulders are facing slightly toward your on side (fig. 15). This rotation, using the strong muscles of the back and abdomen, is what powers a classic canoe forward stroke.

Many paddlers try to involve the torso muscles by bobbing—alternately leaning forward and sitting up. Two problems

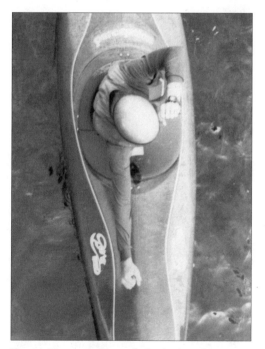

Fig. 14. *Torso rotation at the beginning of a canoe forward stroke. Note the shoulders are nearly in line with the long axis of the boat. (Top arm is bent more than it would normally be at the catch of a forward stroke.)* Bruce Lessels

Fig. 15. *After unwinding your torso, your shoulders should face forward again or slightly toward your on side.* Bruce Lessels

arise from bobbing: The bow constantly rises and falls in the water, slowing the boat; and every time you sit up, causing your hips to thrust the boat forward, you have to lean forward again, checking the boat's momentum.

To keep from bobbing, maintain a constant forward lean of about ten degrees while rotating your torso. Sit comfortably upright, being careful to avoid slouching, since it impairs your ability to twist. Some paddlers consciously arch their backs during the wind up phase of the stroke, letting their spines straighten during the power phase. This allows them to get a little extra reach with their bottom arms at the catch.

To see how important the first part of your forward stroke is, reach your bottom arm out straight toward the bow and rotate your shoulders so they face toward your off side, as described above under the setup. Note where the fingers of your bottom hand touch the boat. Now unwind your torso, keeping your arm out straight, and note where your hand touches the boat at the end of this phase. From here to the first point on the boat is the extent of your torso twist—only about fifteen to eighteen inches—so efficiency is of the essence.

The arms. Go back to the position where your shoulders are in line with the long axis of the boat and your torso is facing toward your off side. Extend your top arm with a slight comfortable bend in the elbow and your hand at about eye level or slightly higher. Extend your bottom arm out straight in front of you. Now grasp your paddle. You're at the catch (fig. 16). Your bottom arm is perfectly straight, which provides maximum extension on your stroke and transmits the power of your torso twist through bones and tendons rather than muscles. Your top arm is comfortably bent at the elbow to allow your top hand to get out over the water on your on side. This keeps your stroke parallel to the keel and as close as possible to the boat's centerline, to ensure that the power you deliver propels you straight ahead, rather than turning you.

Now unwind your torso, keeping your bottom arm extended while your top arm is driving down and straightening (fig. 17). When you have used up your torso twist, begin to bend your bottom arm slightly to facilitate removing the paddle from the water. Bending your bottom arm does not generate addi-

Fig. 16. *At the catch of a canoe forward stroke. Lower arm is straight, top arm is comfortably bent, and shoulders are rotated away from the on side.* Karen Blom

Fig. 17. *The power phase of the canoe forward stroke. The lower arm is still straight and the shoulders have unwound.* Karen Blom

tional pull on the paddle but simply allows it to continue moving at the same speed as the boat, so you can remove it from the water without checking the boat's motion.

Recover by dropping your top hand slightly to your off side and lifting up slightly with your bottom hand (fig. 18). You only need to recover the paddle an inch above the surface of the

Fig. 18. *Recovering between forward strokes by dropping the top hand and lifting with the bottom hand.* Karen Blom

water. Saving a few inches of arm movement on each stroke can mean a significant energy savings if you multiply it over a few thousand strokes a day. Once the blade is clear of the water, straighten your bottom arm and raise your top hand again to return to the catch of the next stroke.

Forward stroke corrections. Beginners sometimes find it frustrating trying to paddle straight, since whitewater canoes turn so easily. For a solo canoeist nearly every stroke will need a correction to offset its turning effect on the boat. With a stroke on each side, tandem paddlers won't need as many corrections, but one paddler nearly always overpowers the other, so corrections are needed.

There are three correction strokes available to canoeists: the pry, the j stroke, and the perk, or off-side forward stroke. The perk is described under "Canoe Strokes" (see page 33). Here are the pry and j stroke, which are tacked onto the end of a forward stroke.

The pry is the easiest correction to learn and often the most powerful. At the end of a forward stroke turn your top wrist so that the thumb is facing back toward you (fig. 19). Make sure your top hand begins out over the edge of your boat in the same vertical plane as your bottom hand. Your blade should

Fig. 19. *A pry correction used to steer a solo canoe. Note the top-hand thumb is pointing up.* Karen Blom

start against the side of your boat. Now pull across your body with the top hand, using the edge of your boat as a fulcrum. The pull across should be quick and powerful in order to minimize the amount of time you spend correcting. The pry should be a short, quick stroke. If you let the blade get too far from the boat, it will cause unnecessary drag, and you will lose speed quickly.

A stern paddler using a pry correction in a tandem boat should try to keep pace with the bow paddler so their strokes hit at the same time. He may have to adjust his rhythm to accommodate the bow paddler by either shortening his forward stroke so he has time to pry, making his pries very quick, or skipping a stroke once in a while and falling back into the rhythm on the next stroke.

The j stroke, while somewhat difficult to master, is more efficient than the pry, because it uses the same face of the blade as the forward stroke, so it can be incorporated more smoothly into the motion of a forward stroke. Start rotating your top wrist so your thumb faces away from you as you finish unwinding your torso on a forward stroke (fig. 20). As with the pry, your top hand should start out over the water on your paddle side. To correct with a j stroke, pull your top hand slightly to your off side, using the edge of the boat as a fulcrum. Your bot-

Fig. 20. *A j stroke used to steer a solo canoe. Note the top-hand thumb is pointing down, and the top hand is out over the gunwale.* Karen Blom

tom hand should grip the shaft loosely, allowing it to turn as you rotate your top wrist. Your bottom wrist should stay straight throughout the j stroke, to reduce fatigue.

On an ideal j correction, steering takes place throughout the forward stroke, so you pause imperceptibly at the end of each stroke. However, this takes many years to master. A few common mistakes on the j stroke are:

1. Failing to keep the blade buried in the water throughout the stroke. This often results from prematurely dropping your top hand forward and down, as you would on the recovery phase of the stroke. This causes your blade to move back and out of the water. To correct this, keep your top hand high and out over the gunwale for as long as you want the correction to be effective.

2. Failing to turn your top wrist enough so that the blade never becomes parallel to the boat and doesn't provide an effective correction. This may be due to a lack of wrist flexibility and can be corrected by changing your top-hand grip slightly, so the thumb is turned more toward the bow of the boat as shown in figure 21. With this modified grip, you can

Fig. 21. *An alternative grip that reduces the amount of wrist flexibility necessary for j stroke corrections.* Karen Blom

push the on side of the t grip forward with your top thumb to bring the blade more parallel to the boat.

3. Doing the j stroke with your bottom hand, rather than your top hand. This causes fatigue and is far less effective than doing the j stroke with your top hand while letting your bottom hand grip the paddle loosely. Try holding the paddle more loosely in your bottom hand, or even let go with your bottom hand when the edge of the boat is being used as a fulcrum.

4. Failing to reach over the on-side gunwale with the top hand so it is in the same vertical plane as the bottom hand. This reduces the power of a j stroke by lifting the blade out of the water. Be sure your top hand is directly above your bottom hand when initiating a j stroke.

A subtle, but no less effective, steering technique for forward paddling is leaning. Because the bow of a whitewater boat is wedge-shaped, sinking more of one side of the wedge into the water (by leaning to that side) will drive the boat the other way. If you want to steer left, lean right, and vice versa. The difficulty with using leans to steer is that they must be subtle. You need to develop a very sensitive touch, so you can feel when the boat picks up turning momentum in one direction or the other and counteract it by leaning appropriately.

Combining j strokes and boat leans is the most efficient way to paddle in a straight line. A small correction on every stroke is preferable to a big correction on every fourth or fifth stroke, since smaller corrections slow the boat much less than larger ones.

Canoe forward sweep

The forward sweep stroke turns the boat and adds speed. This can be very useful on whitewater, where momentum is often at a premium. The forward sweep is similar to a forward stroke. You place the paddle in the water at the front of the boat and remove it toward the stern. However, the paddle in a sweep stroke is held more horizontally by keeping the top hand low over the deck of the boat.

Start your sweep stroke by fully extending your bottom arm forward, keeping your top hand low (fig. 22). Reach as far

Fig. 22. *Setting up for a forward sweep in an OC-1. Bottom arm is straight, and top arm is low.* Karen Blom

forward as you comfortably can by rotating your torso as you would for the setup of a forward stroke. Place the paddle in the water from this position, and sweep as wide an arc away from the boat as possible, finishing the stroke just before the paddle hits the boat behind you (fig. 23). The farther the blade is from

Fig. 23. *Completing a forward sweep stroke. The bottom arm is still extended, and the shoulders have completed their unwinding so they are now facing the on side. The wake the paddle has created in the water shows the path of the stroke.* Karen Blom

the center of the boat during the stroke the better, since this gives the paddle the maximum possible turning leverage.

Unweighting the bow when doing a sweep makes the boat easier to turn. To do this, use a less-horizontal shaft angle—about forty-five degrees to the water—to lift the bow while you are turning.

The sweep stroke described above is most often used in a solo canoe. Tandem paddlers usually use only the first or last half of this stroke, since their position in the boat causes the other half to draw the boat sideways rather than turning it. In the bow of a tandem canoe, use the first half of the sweep, completing it when the paddle reaches a position even with your hip. In the stern, place the paddle in the water even with your hip, and do only the back half of the stroke.

Canoe reverse sweep

The reverse sweep is great when you need to turn sharply and are not concerned about conserving momentum but tends to be overused by solo canoeists who are unsure of their cross sweep (see page 33), and tandem paddlers who could get away with a pry. The problem with the reverse sweep is that it stops the boat dead, or moves it slightly backwards, while turning it.

The reverse sweep is the opposite of the forward sweep. Start with the paddle next to the boat behind you, your bottom arm straight and shoulders rotated toward your paddle side. Now unwind your shoulders while describing a wide arc away from the boat with your paddle. Stop just before hitting the boat in front of you and remove the blade by lifting up slightly on your bottom hand. Again, solo paddlers will use the entire stroke, while bow tandem paddlers will use only the last half of the stroke, and stern tandem paddlers will use only the first half of the stroke.

Canoe draw stroke

A draw stroke pulls the boat, or your end of the boat, directly to the side using the powerful torso muscles. Arch your top arm just in front of and higher than your forehead with the hand in front of your opposite shoulder and out over the gunwale fig. 24.) Hold the t grip in your top hand and let the paddle hang vertically. To get the most out of your trunk muscles, rotate your

Fig. 24. *A draw stroke in a solo canoe. Note the boat is moving directly sideways toward the paddle.* Noland Hisey

torso so your shoulders face toward the paddle. Now place your lower hand on the shaft with the elbow partly flexed. Fix your arms in this position and see how much motion you can achieve by bending your trunk sideways, as if you were trying to touch your shoulder to your same-side hip. Some power comes by pushing down with the upper arm as well. The muscles of the shaft arm fix the pivot point. They do not actively pull.

While the blade usually moves straight toward the centerline of the boat in a draw, you can position the stroke farther forward or back by rotating your torso to face the stern or the bow, adding either a back stroke or a forward stroke component to it.

Canoe duffek stroke

Named for expatriate Czech paddler Milo Duffek, this is an aggressive stroke that allows you to turn the boat while maintaining forward momentum. The British call it a bow rudder, which is perhaps more descriptive of its purpose, but since it is usually referred to in the United States as a duffek, that name will be used here.

To get into the duffek position, hold the paddle blade out to the side at chest level with your hands in front of your body. Rotate your wrists and your elbows up and backward until the normal power face of your blade faces forward instead of aft.

Fig. 25. *A duffek stroke in a solo canoe. The top arm is in a low position that protects the paddler's shoulders but is not as effective in turning the boat as a slightly higher position would be.* Noland Hisey

The thumb of the grip hand will point straight down just next to your face. Now bring your top hand across your body so that it's almost touching the opposite shoulder and you can "read your watch" when looking at the blade (fig. 25). Lower the shaft elbow until its forearm is horizontal. Now rotate your torso so your shoulders are facing in the direction of the turn. This shoulder rotation is called "loading" and sets up the powerful muscles of your torso to transfer force to the stroke. Some paddlers place their grip hands behind their heads for added leverage, but this extreme position can cause dislocation if your shoulders are not used to it. Turn the boat by allowing your torso to unwind so your bow is pulled toward the paddle. Be careful to take the paddle out of the water just before it hits the boat to avoid tripping over it.

Duffeks are done either in the bow of a tandem canoe or in a solo canoe and can be dynamic or static, meaning that the paddle can be pulled through the water causing the boat to turn as described above, or the motion of the water or the boat, with a stationary paddle blade, can cause you to turn (fig. 26).

You can also employ an open or closed blade angle in a duffek to vary the amount of turning force delivered by the stroke. In an open duffek, place the paddle in the water farther

Fig. 26. *A static duffek used to change the boat's angle on a wave. The top arm is in a higher position here than in figure 25.* Noland Hisey

back and out to the side. This stroke will have a maximum turning effect on the boat but, because of the drag created by the blade angle, will slow the boat considerably. A closed duffek, on the other hand, starts with the blade close to the bow of the boat and allows you to maintain most of your momentum while turning gradually. You should practice open, closed, and all the duffeks in-between so you have the proper one at your disposal when the need arises.

Canoe cross strokes

Cross strokes involve using the paddle on your off side without changing your grip. They are used primarily by solo canoeists and bow paddlers in tandem, although some unorthodox sternmen use them occasionally as well. Crossing over the boat may at first seem like more trouble than it's worth, especially if your upper body is not very flexible. Why not just switch paddle sides by trading top hand for bottom hand?

There are several schools of thought on switching paddling sides in a canoe. Purists believe you should never do it, since it is "bad" technique. Others switch once in a while, and some paddlers switch every few strokes. There are plenty of great paddlers in each category, but there are some distinct disadvantages to switching too often. First, during the switch you are vulnerable. Even the best switchers miss once in a while, and if it happens to be in the midst of a turbulent rapid, the missed switch could have wet consequences. Secondly, switching is sometimes used as a substitute for learning cross strokes and, as such, can become a crutch. Last, but certainly not least, cross strokes are among the great techniques of canoeing, adding to its grace as well as its challenge and allure; by switching, you miss out on this technique.

Cross draw. The cross draw is one of the easiest cross strokes to learn and is the most used since it is the primary method of pulling the bow of a solo or tandem boat toward the paddler's off side. To start, bring your top hand down and place it as if you were about to reach into a slightly high jacket pocket. Your t grip thumb should be pointed upward. Now bring your bottom hand across the boat in front of you and choke up on the shaft. Reach the paddle as far away from the boat on your off side as possible by rotating your shoulders toward that side. Now place the blade in the water and allow your shoulders to unrotate until the blade comes close to the side of the boat (fig. 27). Recover the paddle just before it hits the boat by dropping your t-grip hand and slightly raising your shaft hand.

A variation on the cross draw involves bringing your top hand up high above your off-side ear (fig. 28). Again rotate your torso toward your off side, and place the paddle in the water as far away from the boat as possible. This variation will turn you as well as giving you some support.

Cross forward stroke. Solo canoeists may hate to admit it, but there are times when every one of them wishes he had a blade on the other side to pick up speed as quickly and easily as a kayaker. Cross forward strokes fill this gap by allowing you to accelerate from a standstill or in situations where your momentum is turning you toward your off side. Practice cross forward strokes so they become comfortable and you feel confident with them in whitewater. The use of them is one of the primary differences between good and excellent solo paddlers.

First, cross over the boat with both arms fully extended, both wrists straight, and your t-grip thumb facing toward your

Fig. 27. *Cross draw technique in a solo canoe. The shoulders have been rotated toward the off side, and the bottom arm is fully extended.* Noland Hisey

Fig. 28. *A high cross draw. The t-grip hand is much higher than in figure 27, allowing the blade to support more weight but reducing its turning effect.* Bruce Lessels

on side. It helps to choke up on the paddle somewhat. Now lean forward and drive down on the paddle with your top hand, while pulling back with your bottom arm (fig. 29). End the stroke just in front of your hips, and recover either by feath-

Fig. 29. *Cross forward stroke technique on flatwater. The lower hand is choked up on the paddle shaft considerably, making the stroke more comfortable.* Noland Hisey

Fig. 30. *An in-water recovery. Moving from one cross forward stroke to the next by feathering the blade back to the catch.* Noland Hisey

ering (slicing the blade through the water at an angle that provides the least possible resistance) back to the catch (fig. 30) or by lifting your bottom hand up and forward to return the paddle to your on side.

Cross forward strokes are not as powerful as on-side forward strokes, so they should be used only where necessary. Try to get back to your on side as soon as possible. Also, the biomechanics of cross forward strokes force you to lean forward, causing the bow to dive, so on certain moves you may have to do without them, instead relying on j-stroke corrections or a well-timed push off a rock.

The perk. Combining cross forward strokes with on-side forward strokes is called the perk, after southern racer Randy Perkins. It allows you to paddle forward without j strokes or pry corrections and is the fastest forward stroke over short distances available to solo canoeists. Practice the perk using various combinations of on-side and off-side forward strokes, e.g., 1-to-1, 2-to-1, 3-to-1, etc., to see which is most effective for you in a particular boat.

Cross forward sweep. Otherwise known as the pretzel stroke, the cross forward sweep is difficult to master, but it is essential to good solo canoeing since it allows you to initiate a turn toward your on side while at the same time giving your boat forward momentum.

To do a cross forward sweep, first get into the same position as in the cross forward stroke. Now move your top hand down and toward your on side, while moving your bottom hand toward your off side. Now pull back and across your body with your bottom hand while driving forward with your top hand (fig. 31). If you feel like a pretzel, it's working!

Because of the unusual flexibility required for the cross forward sweep, some people have trouble putting much power into it. One key is to make sure the stroke is moving through the water faster than the boat is already moving when you do the stroke. To understand this concept, try a cross forward sweep from a dead stop. It will turn the boat easily toward your on side. Now take a few strokes forward to pick up some momentum and try the cross forward sweep moving the paddle through the water at the same speed as the first time. The

Fig. 31. *The cross forward sweep showing the hand position and the flexibility required.* Bruce Lessels

boat will not react to the stroke unless the paddle is accelerating through the water and getting ahead of the speed of the boat.

Back paddling

Back paddling accounts for a small percentage of the strokes taken by most canoeists in an average day's paddle. Its importance comes not from the frequency with which it is used but from the urgency with which it is sometimes needed. When you find yourself unexpectedly backward in a difficult drop, it is often impractical to turn around. The only option is to continue backing down the rapid using the variety of techniques explained below. Practice back paddling on flatwater and down easy rapids to build your comfort with back strokes, so when you need them they come to you easily.

Straight back stroke. The simplest back stroke is the opposite of a forward stroke. Start the blade in the water next to or slightly behind your hip with your shoulders rotated toward your paddle side. Your top thumb should face toward your paddle side, and you should be using the back face of the blade as the power face. Now unwind your shoulders while driving your bottom arm forward and keeping your top hand over the water (the paddle shaft is vertical). To recover, drop your top hand down and toward your off side while lifting up slightly with your bottom hand.

Compound back stroke. For back paddling long distances, or maneuvering while paddling backward, the compound back stroke is ideal, since it makes it easy to vary your course and to look behind you in the direction you're heading. It is especially effective when you need precise control while paddling backward.

To begin the compound back stroke, rotate your shoulders toward your on side and look at your stern grab loop. Now place your paddle in the water behind you with the power face facing forward and your top thumb facing toward your off side (fig. 32). Initiate the stroke by unwinding your shoulders until the paddle is about parallel to your hip. At this point, switch power faces by rotating both wrists so that your top thumb faces toward your on side. Continue with a straight back stroke until you reach the bow, where a reverse j correction ends the stroke.

To do the reverse j, turn your top thumb back toward you at the end of the back stroke, and pry off the edge of the boat toward the bow (fig. 33). This bow pry is similar in principle to the stern pry described on page 21. Your top hand begins out

Fig. 32. *At the catch of a compound back stroke.* Karen Blom

Fig. 33. *A reverse j stroke at the end of a compound back stroke.* Karen Blom

over your bottom hand, and you use the edge of the boat for leverage. The only difference between the two is the position of the paddle. In the bow pry, the blade is as far forward as possible, while in the stern pry, the blade is as far back as possible.

By varying the angle of your blade at the catch, and adjusting the amount of reverse j at the end of the stroke, you can steer toward or away from your paddle side. Adding a slight draw component at the catch will help you go straight when accelerating backward from a dead stop.

Cross back stroke. The final arrow in your quiver of back strokes should be the cross back stroke. The cross back requires lots of dexterity but comes in handy when you need to paddle backward while resisting a current that is trying to turn your boat to your off side.

Cross the paddle over the bow of your boat, rotating your shoulders so your torso faces toward your off side (fig. 34). Keep rotating until you can see your stern grab loop. Your top thumb should be facing your off side, and your paddle shaft should be vertical. Now unwind your torso, keeping the power face of your paddle perpendicular to the keel line of the boat for as long as possible.

This stroke propels you backward while also turning you toward your off side. It can be used in combination with a straight back stroke in a sort of backward perk for better acceleration.

Fig. 34. *Cross back stroke in a solo canoe.* Karen Blom

Coordinating strokes in a tandem boat

Mastering these strokes alone may make you a proficient solo paddler, but tandem paddlers must also coordinate their efforts so they think and paddle as a team. Two paddlers working together can produce more than the sum of their individual efforts, but two paddlers working independently can produce confusion.

To work together in a canoe, you must think of the entire boat, not just your end. To the bow paddler, this means understanding that although your end has cleared a rock, your partner's end may not have cleared it yet. It also means setting a rhythm with your strokes that the stern paddler can follow, so you both catch at the same time (fig. 35).

To the stern paddler, thinking as a team means following your partner's lead. If he draws to initiate a turn, you should draw as well to complement his stroke, since in order to spin the boat to the right, you must turn your end to the left, and vice versa (fig. 36). The idea of complementary strokes is sometimes difficult for a stern paddler to grasp, but although counterintuitive, learning to complement the bow paddler's strokes is essential to being able to paddle effectively on whitewater.

The responsibilities of the two partners need to be determined ahead of time so that decisions can be made quickly and communicated clearly. Their tasks can be characterized by the range of each paddler's vision. The bow paddler is responsible for the short-term course. He looks for small rocks that may not

Fig. 35. *Hitting together on each stroke is essential in a tandem boat.* Jim Gariepy

Fig. 36. *The stern paddler is complementing the bow paddler's duffek with a forward sweep.* Noland Hisey

be visible to the stern paddler and initiates eddy turns after the stern paddler has taken care of the approach. Again complementing the bow paddler's efforts, the stern paddler plans the long-term course. He sets the line into eddies and determines the general route down a rapid.

STROKES FOR KAYAK

The control hand

Most kayak paddles are asymmetrical. Both blades are curved and they are offset from one another on the shaft. The curve, or spoon shape, of the blade helps it "grip" the water. The offset reduces wind resistance from the nonactive blade and puts a kayaker's wrists in a natural position when paddling. The amount of offset varies from forty-five degrees to ninety degrees depending on personal preference. While eighty-five to ninety degrees was the standard offset until a short time ago, many kayakers have recently begun using paddles with offsets of seventy-five degrees or less to reduce wrist fatigue. As a result of the offset between blades, and the asymmetrical shape of the blades, paddles can be made with the blades facing in either of two orientations. They are classified as either left-hand control or right-hand control.

To account for the offset, you need to rotate the paddle shaft, positioning one blade, and then the other, to take a stroke (figs. 37 and 38). One hand acts as the control hand, remaining firmly on the shaft, while the other hand allows the shaft to rotate within it. There are as many theories about how to deter-

Fig. 37. *A right-hand-control paddle in position for a stroke on the right side. The concave face of the right blade is facing the paddler with his right wrist straight.* Karen Blom

Fig. 38. *With the right wrist cocked back, the shaft is rotated so the left blade is set up to take a stroke. Note the left wrist remains straight.* Karen Blom

mine control hands as there are paddlers, but most people can learn to control the paddle with either hand. The majority of kayakers use right-hand-control paddles. There is an advantage to following the pack, since it is much easier to find right-hand-control paddles than left-hand-control paddles in retail stores, or to borrow one from a friend when yours breaks.

By maintaining a firm grip with the control hand, you always know where both blades are. This becomes very important, especially when rolling, bracing, or running difficult whitewater where you can't be preoccupied with keeping track of your paddle blades. Most paddle shafts are oval, with the long axis of the oval perpendicular to the flat of the blade. By holding this long axis in the crotch between your thumb and index finger, you can quickly relocate your control hand if it slips. If your paddle shaft is not oval, you can easily add an oval to the control-hand side by cutting a thin strip of minicell foam and taping it to the surface of the shaft that's in line with the power face of the control-hand blade.

Kayak forward stroke

With blades on both sides of the boat, correction strokes are not necessary to make a kayak go in a straight line. Also, the power phase of one stroke is the recovery phase of the next. This makes a kayak forward stroke more efficient than a canoe forward stroke. However, as with the canoe forward stroke, proper technique requires lots of practice.

Sitting comfortably upright in your boat with a straight spine and a slight forward lean, rotate your torso away from the active side, and extend your active arm forward, keeping it perfectly straight (fig. 39). Your nonactive hand should be at about eye level or slightly higher, and your nonactive arm should be slightly bent. Now place your active blade in the water and unrotate your torso (fig. 40.) At the end of your torso rotation, allow the paddle to continue moving through the water by bending your bottom arm slightly. Simultaneously lower your top hand to begin to lift the paddle out of the water for the

Fig. 39. *The catch of a kayak forward stroke.* Karen Blom

Fig. 40. *Power phase of a kayak forward stroke. Note shoulder rotation and top hand position.* Karen Blom

recovery (fig. 41). The power phase of the stroke should end just in front of the cockpit, and the blade should be clear of the water by the time the paddle reaches your hips.

Effective torso rotation during a kayak forward stroke requires loose hamstrings to keep from slouching, which adds a curve to your spine and hinders rotation. Toe touches are a good way to develop this flexibility.

Flatwater racers and some whitewater paddlers get extra power out of a forward stroke by pumping with their legs inside the boat. As you take a stroke on one side, push on the opposite foot pedal. This pumping motion complements your torso rotation.

To steer while paddling forward, focus your vision on a point on shore and paddle toward it (don't look at the boat or

Fig. 41. *The recovery phase of the forward stroke. The bottom arm is bent and the top hand has dropped to remove the blade from the water.* Karen Blom

the paddle!). Incorporate small sweeps or stern draws (see pages 44 and 48) into your forward stroke every time you begin to veer off course. The key is to take many small steering strokes, correcting early and often. You can feel the boat going off-line with your hips. When you start to veer off course even a degree, immediately incorporate a slight sweep into your next stroke on the side toward which you are turning.

Each time you use a correcting sweep, you will need a countersweep on the other side on the next stroke, since every correction will overcompensate slightly. Eventually, these corrections should be integrated smoothly into your forward stroke rhythm so they don't interrupt the cadence.

Kayak forward sweep

The most basic turning stroke in a kayak is the forward sweep. This stroke turns you as it propels you forward and is especially important for aggressive paddling techniques.

Start by holding the paddle low across the front deck. Now extend your straight bottom arm forward on your active side and rotate your shoulders so your torso is facing away from that side. Place your active blade in the water right next to the boat at the paddle's fullest extension (fig. 42) and sweep an arc from front to back, keeping the blade as far away from you as possible throughout the stroke (fig. 43). Watch the tip of the blade to help bring your torso into play, and maintain a straight bottom arm throughout the stroke to transmit power directly to the paddle. Keep your top hand low over the deck of the boat to ensure as horizontal a paddle shaft as possible, and be sure the blade remains buried in the water during the stroke.

For a more powerful finish, drive your top hand across your chest at the end of the stroke (fig. 44). This will drive the blade forcefully into the boat at the stern, using the bottom hand as a fulcrum.

Fig. 42. *The catch of a kayak forward sweep.* Karen Blom

Fig. 43. *The power phase of the forward sweep.* Karen Blom

Fig. 44. *Driving across the body with the top arm at the end of a forward sweep. Note the head and shoulder rotation.* Karen Blom

Kayak reverse sweep

The reverse sweep is the most effective technique for sharp turns, but it also slows your boat. Beginners commonly use it in place of a forward sweep on the opposite side of the boat, because it offers extra turning leverage. Yet while it is an effective turning stroke, the reverse sweep keeps your boat from gaining the momentum that is crucial to such moves as eddy turns, peelouts, and ferries. It is most effective when you must turn on a dime and momentum is not a concern.

Reverse sweep technique is similar to forward sweep technique except that the blade moves from the back to the front of the boat. Keeping your hands low, reach behind you and rotate your shoulders to face the active side (fig. 45). Keeping a straight bottom arm, unwind your torso as you trace a wide arc toward the bow (fig. 46). End the stroke just before the blade hits the front of the boat.

By angling the active blade at forty-five degrees to the water's surface, you can also push down on the water, giving yourself a brace that will support some weight while you turn. This hybrid stroke is useful in backing out of holes and entering turbulent eddies.

Fig. 45. *Starting a reverse sweep with a straight bottom arm and shoulders rotated.* Bruce Lessels

Fig. 46. *The power phase of the reverse sweep. Note the paddler is still watching the blade, and the nonactive hand remains low over the front deck.* Bruce Lessels

Kayak draw

The draw stroke moves your boat laterally across the water, allowing you to avoid a rock quickly or adjust your position slightly when entering an eddy. Pulling a kayak directly sideways moves the boat in the direction of greatest resistance, so it is not an effective technique over large distances, but the draw stroke comes in handy when quick, minor corrections are needed.

Hold the paddle vertically next to you and rotate your torso to face the active blade. Both hands should be out over the water with your top hand directly over your bottom hand (fig. 47). The power face of the active blade should face toward you. Now drive down with the top hand while pulling in with the bottom arm. The top hand acts as a fulcrum. By leaning your boat away from the active blade, you can reduce the amount of drag on your hull, allowing it to slip more easily sideways through the water. Note how the dynamic equilibrium set up by leaning away from the draw actually adds to your stability.

You can use either an in-water or out-of-water recovery for the draw stroke. The in-water recovery starts with you flexing both wrists to rotate the blade ninety degrees so it can be sliced away from the boat to the beginning of the next stroke. When

Fig. 47. *A draw to the side showing hand, arm, and torso positions.*
Bruce Lessels

feathering the blade away from the boat, be careful to maintain a constant angle that minimizes resistance in the water. Several factors affect the ease of feathering: blade shape and thickness, current direction around your boat, and your dexterity. Practice feathering by paddling around an obstacle course on only one blade, keeping it in the water for the entire course.

The out-of-water recovery allows you to go to a different stroke more quickly than the in-water recovery but is more awkward when going from one draw stroke to another. Drop your top hand forward and lift your bottom hand slightly up and back. It is not necessary to feather the blade on this recovery.

Kayak stern draw

The stern draw is really just the last, and most powerful, half of a forward sweep. While not a distinctly different stroke, it is treated separately from the forward sweep to emphasize its importance.

Fig. 48. *A stern draw used to maintain angle while crossing a current.* Karen Blom

From the draw position described above, drop your top hand forward and bring your bottom hand back with a straight bottom arm so your paddle is in the water behind you at about four o'clock or eight o'clock. Your shoulders should be facing somewhat toward your active side. Now using the rotation still left in your torso and driving your top arm across your chest, draw the blade in toward the stern (fig. 48).

Kayak duffek

Milo Duffek is perhaps the best-known historic figure in paddling because of his adaptation of a flatwater turning stroke for whitewater. The duffek, or, as the British call it, the bow rudder, is a way to guide a turn with the paddle in the aggressive forward position. For the beginner, the hand position in a duffek stroke can be somewhat awkward. As the stroke becomes more familiar, however, it will begin to feel more natural.

To get into a duffek position, hold the paddle horizontal at shoulder level in front of your body. Cock both wrists back toward your body as far as possible. Your active blade's power face should now be facing forward. Maintain this wrist position and swing the inactive arm up and across your forehead as if

Fig. 49. *A "cruising" duffek with low top arm. Blade angle is open, causing the boat to turn sharply.* Noland Hisey

Fig. 50. *A "racing" duffek with high top arm. Blade angle is closed, causing the boat to turn over a wide radius.* Bruce Lessels

you were going to read your watch, so that your top and bottom hands are both over the water on the active side of your boat. Figures 49 and 50 show a range of duffek positions. The position you use is a matter of body type, flexibility, and personal style. Rotate your torso toward your active side, causing your active blade to move away from the edge of your boat. When your blade is about two feet from the boat, drop it into the water and untwist your torso, keeping your bottom arm as nearly straight as possible until your blade almost hits the boat in front of you.

The most common method for finishing the duffek is to turn it into a forward stroke by rolling both wrists forward, so your active blade's power face is facing back toward you and pulling on it as a forward stroke. This is especially useful for accelerating out of a turn you have just completed or stopping the momentum of a turn.

As with the draw, both in-water and out-of-water recoveries are possible with the duffek. The in-water recovery is similar to that described for the draw and is used to go from one duffek stroke to another. Rotate both wrists forward and move the blade out to the beginning of the next stroke by again rotating your torso toward your active side until your blade is at about two o'clock. To do the out-of-water recovery, lift up and forward with your bottom arm, causing the blade to lift out of the water toward the bow.

A duffek can be either active, as described above, or static, acting as a bow rudder. In the active duffek, the boat turns because of the movement of the paddle through the water. In a static duffek, the paddle remains stationary and the boat turns because of its movement relative to the water.

To see how the static duffek works, hold your paddle in the water in duffek position and have a friend push your boat forward. The movement of the boat will cause it to turn, since the static duffek is acting as a rudder. Of course, once your momentum dies, the static duffek stops having any turning effect on the boat. You can do the same thing without your friend by taking a few strokes forward to gain momentum and suddenly placing a duffek in the water on one side. Again, the static blade will act as a rudder in the bow.

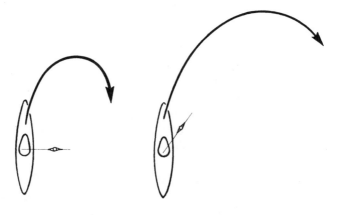

OPEN ANGLE   CLOSED ANGLE

Fig. 51. *Open and closed blade angles on a duffek. Note the tighter turn made possible by a more open blade angle and the more gradual arc that results from a closed angle.* Noland Hisey

To combine static and active duffeks, take several strokes forward, then sweep on one side, and do a static duffek on the other. When you feel the boat start to lose momentum, actively draw the duffek in toward the bow. Just before your paddle hits the bow, roll your wrists forward and turn it into a forward stroke by pulling the blade toward you.

The angle of the duffek relative to the keel line of the boat is important in determining how quickly you turn and how much momentum you maintain through the turn (fig. 51). A small, or closed, angle will allow you to maintain more momentum but will turn you in a wide arc. On the other hand, a larger, or more open, angle will turn you very quickly but will also slow the boat significantly.

Sometimes it may be best to insert the paddle in a neutral position, i.e., parallel to the keel line, then open it into a duffek position at the precise moment it's needed. Practice all variations, so you'll have the right one ready when you need it.

Kayak back stroke

As in a canoe, there are times when back strokes come in handy in a kayak: When you want to come to a sudden stop, a few well-timed back strokes will kill your momentum; back ferrying in the flatwater above a drop is often the best way to scout; and when you get turned around in whitewater, backing down a rapid for a short distance may be the most practical way to get back on track.

Back stroke mechanics are the opposite of forward stroke mechanics. Start with your torso rotated toward the active side and your active arm slightly bent in order to place the paddle in the water at your hip. Your top arm should be comfortably bent at eye level. Now unwind your torso, using the back face of the active blade as the power face (fig. 52). When you reach full rotation of your torso and full extension of your active arm, drop your top hand and raise your bottom arm, lifting the active blade out of the water and setting the nonactive blade for the next stroke. It is generally easiest to look over only one shoulder (fig. 53), but some paddlers prefer to alternate shoulders in certain circumstances.

Fig. 52. *Back paddling in a kayak.* Bruce Lessels

Fig. 53. *It's usually easiest to look over only one shoulder when back paddling.*
David Eden

Ruddering

The stern rudder stroke is very useful when surfing a wave, since it allows you to control the angle of the boat without losing much speed.

To do a rudder, first paddle forward a few strokes to pick up speed. Then place the paddle in the water behind you with both hands over the active side of the boat and the blade almost touching the boat behind you (fig. 54). The blade should be nearly parallel to the keel line and the concave face should be facing the boat. By slightly varying the angle of the blade, you can change the amount the boat turns. You can also add to the

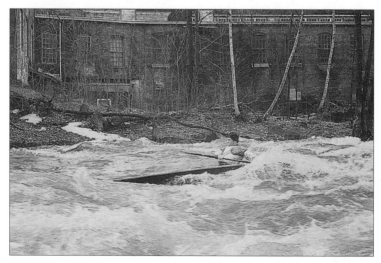

Fig. 54. *A stern rudder used to surf a wave.* Bruce Lessels

turning effect the rudder has on the boat by leaning away from it with a j lean as described in chapter 4.

Improving paddle dexterity

None of the strokes described in this chapter is ever used alone on whitewater. Each move on a river is a series of interconnected paddle motions that guide the boat where you want it to go. The best way to practice linking strokes is to set up situations on flatwater or easy whitewater that require you to use your paddle in unusual positions.

Paddling with only one blade at a time (fig. 55) works on feathering, blade angle, and balance, since it places you in some awkward positions not normally encountered by kayakers (welcome to the world of canoeing). Don't be afraid to use cross strokes as described under canoe techniques above.

The sweep/duffek game is also useful for improving dexterity and getting used to the duffek position. Start with a forward sweep on one side followed by a duffek on the other. Convert your duffek back into a forward sweep by rolling your wrists forward and down at the end of the stroke, and follow it with a duffek on the first side... and so on. These are just a couple of games. Feel free to invent your own.

Fig. 55. *Paddling with only one blade at a time forces you into positions that test your dexterity and balance.* Bruce Lessels

Chapter Three

Leans and Braces

Proper boat lean allows you to vary the effect the river has on your boat by changing the hull shape you present to the current. Boat leans keep you from flipping when entering or leaving the current; they help steer the boat; they let an open canoeist avoid taking on water in waves; and they are essential for squirts and many other tricks.

Braces are strokes that can save you from flipping when your lean fails or give you a "training wheel" when you're not sure just how much to lean. The former is known as a recovering brace and the latter as a supporting brace. As with the training wheels on a bicycle, supporting braces are best used primarily when learning to paddle. You should try to wean yourself off of them as soon as possible, so your paddle is free to guide or propel the boat as you attempt more advanced moves.

Proper outfitting is essential to controlling your leans and bracing effectively. Several outfitting options are presented in chapter 7, but the important point to keep in mind is that your boat should move together with your lower body. In both canoe and kayak, you should think of wearing your boat rather than sitting in it.

LEANS

There are two ways you can lean in whitewater: rigidly, with your body and boat acting as a single unit, or flexibly, with your upper body remaining balanced while you tilt the boat with your lower body. The first is called the "bell buoy" lean. It ties up your paddle to support the weight of your upper body so you don't flip. The second is known as the j lean and is by far the preferred technique for whitewater paddling. The j lean alone is described in this section. The bell buoy lean is only mentioned here as a technique to avoid using.

J leans

A j lean allows you to tilt your lower body and boat independently of your upper body. This is especially important any time you need to lean to counteract a current and guide or propel your boat with your paddle at the same time. Most boats have a point of secondary stability where they are more or less stable. Beyond this point, they quickly become unstable again. Finding the secondary stability of your boat helps you balance on edge with a minimum of effort.

To do a j lean in a canoe, push down with the knee on the side toward which you are leaning and pull up on the opposite knee (fig. 56). At the same time, keep your body weight centered over the boat by flexing at your midsection so you don't have to support your weight on your paddle.

In a kayak, lift up with one knee and push down on the opposite side of your seat while again maintaining your center of gravity over the center of the boat (fig. 57). It feels almost as if you're climbing up the boat toward the high edge.

Fig. 56. *A j lean in a solo canoe. The head and shoulders are still over the boat's center of gravity.* Noland Hisey

Fig. 57. *An extreme j lean in a kayak. While you may not always want to lean this much, the ability to balance with this much lean is valuable.* Bruce Lessels

To practice j leaning, tilt the boat up until you reach the point of secondary stability and paddle around with this lean as shown in figure 57. Try a variety of strokes and maneuvers, regardless of whether you're leaning into or out of turns. When you get tired leaning on one side, try the other. Most canoeists find it psychologically more difficult to lean toward their off sides, since they don't have a brace (see below) on that side. But getting comfortable with off-side leans is essential to feeling comfortable in a canoe. Kayakers on the other hand often get too used to relying on an ever-present brace on both sides. This exercise helps kayakers learn to lean in balance rather than with the support of their paddles.

BRACES

Bracing in a canoe

Since canoeists only have a brace on one side, they tend to favor that side and lean toward it as a precaution against instability. Try to avoid getting into this habit. It limits your ability to learn off-side leans, which are essential in moves such as wave surfing, off-side peelouts, and off-side eddy turns. Instead, work on developing good balance, effective on-side and off-side braces, and a good roll for when the other two fail.

Canoe low brace. Canoeists generally prefer the low brace over the high brace because of the greater leverage it offers. The high body position and the single-bladed paddle used by canoeists favor the low brace by allowing the canoeist to reach his paddle out over the water easily and place the non–power face flat on the surface.

In the recovering low brace, start with your hands low and your elbows high. Your top thumb should face forward. Rotate your shoulders so they are facing toward your on side. Now place the paddle out over the water far enough that your top hand is outside the gunwale (fig. 58). Your top hand should start out lower than your bottom hand. Set the non–power face of the blade flat on the water.

Now lean out of balance toward your on side keeping a rigid upper body. The instant you begin to catch your weight on the paddle, lift up with your on-side knee and push down with your off-side knee, causing the boat to come back to level (fig. 59). Pull up and in on your top hand, and push down on your bottom hand. At the end of a recovering brace, your top hand will end up just in front of your abdomen.

Fig. 58. *Starting a low brace in a C-1. Note that the t-grip hand is lower than the shaft hand.* Bruce Lessels

Fig. 59. *When the paddle hits the water, drive down with your off-side knee and lift with your on-side knee while driving your head toward the water.* Bruce Lessels

The big key to any brace is what you do with your head. While righting the boat with your knees, bring your head down toward the water on your on side. Keep your head down throughout the brace, recovering it by bringing it low across the front deck at the last moment.

To practice a supporting low brace, build up some forward speed and turn toward your on side. Lean into the turn with the paddle in the position described above, except with your t-grip hand slightly higher than your shaft hand. Rather than pulling up on one hand and pushing down with the other, leave the paddle on the surface of the water, and lean on it slightly. Bevel the blade so the front edge is higher than the back edge. This will cause it to rise as long as your boat maintains speed.

Canoe high brace. The high brace can support a lean while guiding you through a turn at the same time. It is used less in canoe than in kayak, because canoeists sit higher in their boats, which makes the high-brace position considerably less powerful than the low-brace position. Whereas for the low brace, the elbows are held high and the hands low, in the high brace, the positions are reversed. The more vertical blade angle that

Fig. 60. *A high brace used to surf a hole in a C-1. Note elbows are held close to the body to guard against shoulder injuries.* Karen Blom

results does not support weight as well as the horizontal blade angle made possible by the low brace.

To bring your paddle into high-brace position, hold it across the gunwales of the boat in front of you, and move both hands up toward your chest by bending both elbows up. Now extend the paddle to your on side, and place the power face of the blade flat on the water (fig. 60). During the brace, keep your lower elbow forward and down to avoid shoulder dislocation.

Like the low brace, the high brace can act as either a recovering stroke or a supporting stroke. In both variations, the body motions are the same as in the low brace; only the paddle position changes. Since the high brace does not support weight as easily as the low brace, you may not feel comfortable leaning the boat over as far.

Cross brace. The off side is often treated as the canoeist's Achilles' heel, but it need not be completely vulnerable. Cross bracing, while somewhat awkward at first, is an effective way to recover from instability on your off side. Both low and high cross braces are possible, but low cross braces are rarely done,

Fig. 61. *A cross brace used to surf a hole in a C-1.* Karen Blom

Fig. 62. *A low cross brace—only for the very flexible with tough shoulders.*
Karen Blom

since they require extreme flexibility and put the paddler's shoulders at risk for dislocation.

A high cross brace is similar to a cross draw except that you hold your paddle shaft more vertically. This is described as a variation of the cross draw on page 30 and is illustrated in figure 61 which shows a C-1 paddler using a high cross brace while surfing a hole.

The high cross brace will save you only if you catch the flip early enough. If you have the flexibility to do it, the low cross brace can be used to recover from any degree of instability. To do a low cross brace, bring your bottom hand in an arc above your head so the non–power face of the paddle slaps the water on your off side (fig. 62). The instant the blade hits the water, drive your head down toward the surface and bring the boat up with your hips in a powerful C motion similar to that described in the C-to-C kayak roll (see page 126). To recover your head from the water, pull in and slightly up on your top hand and slide your head and upper body along the front deck of your boat. This stroke can only be practiced with full commitment; be ready to roll if it fails.

Righting pry. One more way to save yourself from an imminent off-side flip is the righting pry shown in figure 63. This stroke

Fig. 63. *A righting pry.* Karen Blom

uses the resistance caused by lifting your unfeathered blade up through the water to pull, rather than push, yourself back up.

From the pry position described in the forward stroke section (see page 21), start to lean toward your off side. To right your boat, pull down and in with your top hand while pushing out and up with your bottom hand. At the same time, lift up with your off-side knee and push down with your on-side knee.

Bracing in a kayak

With a double-bladed paddle, a kayaker can brace effectively on either side of the boat. While this is an appropriate response to overleaning or unexpected instability, kayakers often brace through turbulence or across current differentials when proper boat lean and careful balance would suffice. By balancing, rather than bracing, you free your paddle to turn or propel the boat. Yet every boater's balance occasionally fails. This is where braces come into their own. With a properly timed brace you can avoid rolling—which on a cold spring day or in a fast shallow rapid is an unpleasant option.

Kayak high brace. Kayakers use high braces more often than low braces. Because they have a paddle on each side, kayakers can't put their blades as flat to the water as canoeists can in a low brace, and since a kayaker's shoulders do not sit as high as a canoeist's do, with hands in a high brace position, a kayaker's paddle shaft is more nearly horizontal than a canoeist's.

First, hold your paddle across the deck in front of you, then bring your hands up toward your chest by flexing at both elbows. Now extend the paddle away from the boat on the side on which you want to brace (fig. 64), keeping the paddle shaft directly above your elbows. Your control wrist should be rotated back so the active blade is flat to the water. Try not to raise your hands above shoulder level, and keep your elbows in close to your body. This minimizes the risk of shoulder dislocation—a common kayaking injury.

In a recovering high brace, drive your head down the moment your blade contacts the water. At the same time, use your hips to right the boat by pulling up on the on-side knee and pushing down on the opposite side of your seat (fig. 65). After the boat is righted, finish the brace by sitting up.

Fig. 64. *A high brace used to surf a hole in a kayak. Note elbows are low and close to the body to protect the shoulders.* Bruce Lessels

Fig. 65. *A recovering high brace showing the head-down body position and the arm position with the elbows in close to the torso.* Noland Hisey

Fig. 66. *A supporting high brace used as the pivot point on the inside of a turn.* Noland Hisey

In a supporting high brace, place your blade to the side of the boat as described above, and lean the boat toward the blade. As long as you sustain your momentum and maintain a slight bevel on the front edge of the blade as shown in figure 66, your paddle will continue to rise on the surface of the water and support your weight.

Kayak low brace. The kayak low brace is often used for hole surfing and by beginners learning to do eddy turns. It is more effective as a stabilizing stroke than as a recovering stroke. It

Fig. 67. *A recovering low brace. Note elbows are up and paddle shaft is almost resting on the boat's bow deck.* Bruce Lessels

takes less energy and strength than a high brace, making it ideal for resting when surfing a hole.

Set your paddle across the boat in front of you and, with your elbows high, place the active blade flat on the water (fig. 67). The non–power face of the blade contacts the water. The body motions are similar to those used in the high braces both for the recovering low brace and for the supporting low brace. (A supporting low brace can easily be turned into a reverse sweep by allowing the paddle to move slightly behind you and then sweeping forward in an arc as described on page 46.)

Sculling braces. In both canoe and kayak, sculling by moving your paddle back and forth on the surface of the water while keeping the blade at an angle that makes it rise to the surface allows you to maintain a supporting brace when neither the boat nor the current is moving. Sculling also keeps your active blade from sinking below the water when surfing steep holes with very frothy backwashes.

Set your blade on the water in either a high- or a low-brace position. Now angle the blade slightly so the leading edge is higher than the trailing edge. Slide the blade forward in the water a foot or two, change blade angles, and slide the blade back a foot or two (fig. 68). By continuing this motion, you can support yourself almost indefinitely.

Fig. 68. *The motion used to keep the paddle on the surface during a sculling brace.* Noland Hisey

MOVING ON

Now that you can move your boat around on flatwater, lean it as needed, and catch yourself if you begin to flip, you're ready to start learning about whitewater. First we'll look at whitewater anatomy and then start learning how to move on a river using the basic flatwater skills you've already acquired.

Chapter Four

The Shape of the River

Water moving downhill encounters rocks and other obstacles that change its course, add turbulence, and vary its speed to form whitewater. Being able to understand and identify certain common whitewater features lets you use the water to your advantage.

A few basic river-reading rules can help make this confusing subject understandable at first, but these are only general guidelines and cannot substitute for "river sense." This is a sort of sixth sense that lets you know to expect a possible downed tree around the next bend, or a bad pinning rock at the bottom of a steep chute (the water flowing between two rocks or other obstacles). River sense is not magic or ESP. It's being tuned into the slightest current differences or other changes in the river environment that tell you something may not be right. Developing a river sense takes many years and countless river runs. As you develop a better river sense, you will be able to discard some of the rules as too rigid and make individual judgments in each situation. Until you have that experience, however, playing it conservatively and following the generally established rules is the safest way to paddle.

EDDIES
Eddies are produced by the very conditions—strong currents and obstructed passages—that make them useful for running a river. They are small islands of quiet water in the midst of the flood where you can arrest your downstream motion to wait for your companions, stop to assess the water ahead, turn your bow for an upstream crossing, or prepare for a complex maneuver. They are formed where water moving downstream encounters an obstacle such as a rock (fig. 69). On the downstream side of the obstacle, the water moves upstream to fill in behind it.

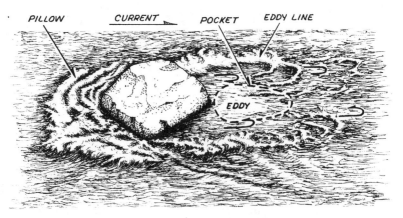

Fig. 69. *Eddy anatomy (see photo of eddy; pg. 6, fig. 5).* Noland Hisey

Where the upstream-moving eddy water meets the downstream current is the eddy line. The tops of the eddy lines in figure 69 appear as whitewater. They extend downstream as less and less distinct divisions between current and eddy water. The eddy line marks a shear zone between two currents that move in opposite directions. Whirlpools and boils of varying size and intensity define this zone. An eddy is strongest right below the obstacle that forms it, weakening the farther downstream

Fig. 70. *Even partly submerged rocks can form eddies.* Bruce Lessels

you go. The area where the eddy water is moving upstream with the most force is called the pocket. This is usually deep in the eddy or next to shore for a shoreline eddy.

The obstacle that forms an eddy is not always directly visible on the surface of the water. Even a rock buried underwater, known as a pourover (see page 75), may form an eddy (fig. 70). Generally, however, the deeper the water flowing over the obstacle, the weaker the eddy it will form. Eddies often form behind holes (see page 75), although stopping in them can be dicey; you must try to sit in the strongest part of the eddy without being sucked up into the hole.

WAVES

One way a river gives off energy is by forming waves. They occur when moving water is compressed into a narrower channel, the gradient of the river bottom changes abruptly, or fast-moving water meets slower-moving water (fig. 71). Waves are fun to paddle through, and they are primarily responsible for the up-and-down movement of whitewater. You can surf a river wave as you would an ocean wave, but since river waves stay in the same place, you can theoretically surf one forever.

Waves have two faces: a steep upstream face and a longer, more gradual downstream face. The pattern of waves in a rapid tells you a tremendous amount about what's going on below the surface. Regular waves generally indicate a deep channel, whereas irregular or choppy waves mean shallower water. A wave train is a series of standing waves that become smaller as you move downstream. One wave out of place in the midst of an otherwise regular-looking rapid may mean an unusually steep or sharp drop just upstream of it.

To punch straight through a wave so it has the least effect on you, paddle at it with your boat pointed perpendicular to it. This does not always mean to orient your boat parallel to the current, since current direction and wave orientation are not necessarily related (fig. 72). Reaching beyond the peak of the wave for a paddle stroke on the downstream face will often help get you over it and will give your paddle the most purchase on the water. Hitting a wave at an angle to it is an invitation to be surfed in the direction the wave is feeding; i.e., a

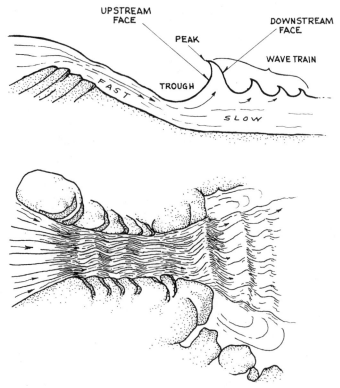

UPSTREAM FACE

DOWNSTREAM FACE

PEAK

WAVE TRAIN

FAST

TROUGH

SLOW

Fig. 71. *Wave anatomy.* John Urban

wave that starts near the river's right shore and angles down-stream toward the center of the river will tend to surf you from river right to river left if you hit it at anything but a ninety-degree angle.

Even very large waves, although they can be intimidating to paddle through, generally present little hazard in themselves. They can block your vision downstream when you are in the troughs and often break on the tops, turning into holes that can temporarily stop or even flip a boat. It is often very difficult to breathe when swimming through long wave trains, however. Time your breathing to take place in the troughs.

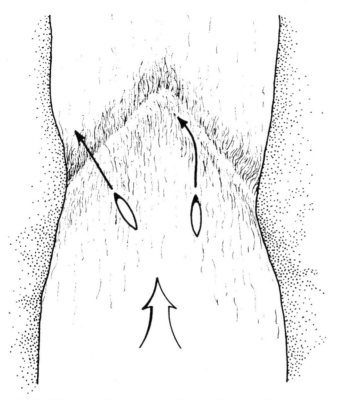

Fig. 72. *Waves are often not oriented perpendicular to the current direction.* Noland Hisey

HOLES

To the uninitiated, holes often look harmless. But while many holes are in fact trivial, some of the most innocuous looking ones are extremely powerful. Holes are also called souse holes, stoppers, hydraulics, pourovers, and reversals. They are formed where water dropping over a ledge or other submerged obstruction forms a frothy backwash. The surface water below the obstruction moves back upstream while the water along the bottom continues to move downstream. Holes can also be thought of as "vertical eddies" or as constantly breaking waves. Figure 6 (page 6) shows a typical hole on a ledgy river. The white froth on the surface is the backwash. Notice that the backwash angles downhill as it moves back into the hole.

To paddle through a hole, use a technique similar to that described above for punching a wave. Maintain an angle perpendicular to the hole and take a powerful stroke on the downstream side of the backwash to pull you through (fig. 73). A hole will hold your boat and turn it sideways if you try to punch it at anything but a ninety-degree angle. This can be fun or terrifying depending on the size of the hole, your skill level, and whether it is intentional or not.

Determining whether a hole is safe or not requires experience and careful observation. The most important factors to consider are: the width and regularity of the backwash, the length of the hole, its shape and size, whether one or both ends are obstructed, the steepness of the water entering the hole, and, most importantly, your skill level.

Holes with strong recirculations are unusual but can be dangerous since they can trap a swimmer, keeping him in the froth below the hole until he is exhausted. Horseshoe-shaped holes can also be nasty, since the current all feeds toward the center of the hole, making it very difficult for a boater or swim-

Fig. 73. *Punching a hole by reaching over the recycle to pull the boat through.* Bruce Lessels

mer to work his way out toward one end or the other. Very regular holes with no current going through them or fluctuations to introduce an element of randomness can exhaust even an upright boater who is having trouble pulling out one end or the other. Holes where both ends are blocked off are especially bad, because the only way out is over or under the recycle. Finally, look out for holes with long backwashes where even a swimmer diving deep to catch the downstream current along the river bottom may not be able to clear the recycle.

POUROVERS

Pourovers are rocks over which a shallow flow of water is running (fig. 74). They typically have holes on the downstream side that can be grabby and dangerous depending on their size. Some pourovers create excellent eddies in which to stop, but the holes below pourovers are generally very steep and difficult to surf, so when stopping behind a pourover, be careful not to get drawn up into the hole. The drop behind a pourover may be as low as a foot or as high as eight to ten feet. A pourover appears from above as a smooth hump of water. Sometimes you see the

Fig. 74. *A side view of a pourover.* Karen Blom

Fig. 75. *The same pourover seen from upstream as it would appear to a boater.*
Bruce Lessels

white froth below the pourover from above, while at other
times you just see the hump and a slight horizon line (fig. 75).

LEDGES

Water running over a ledge generally forms a hole or a wave.
On a river with a ledgy bottom, be on the lookout for dangerous
holes with strong, even recirculations. From upstream, ledges
usually appear as horizon lines across the river. On very high
ledges, or waterfalls, the river below the ledge may not be visible at all. This is a clear signal to scout from shore.

ROCK GARDENS

Rock gardens are rapids with multiple boulders in the river
channel (fig. 76). They can occur on rivers of any difficulty and
are fun places to play, since each boulder creates an eddy.

Rock gardens allow you to "eddy hop." This is a technique
where you run a rapid in small pieces by paddling from eddy to
eddy. It is a good way to scout an unfamiliar rapid from the
river.

Fig. 76. *A typical rock garden.* Bruce Lessels

PILLOWS

A pillow forms above any obstacle where the water rebounds upstream after hitting the obstacle. As the water rebounds it piles up, forming a hump upstream of the obstacle (see figure 69, page 70). This pillow deflects anything floating toward the obstacle, often keeping the two from hitting at all. Rocks with well-developed pillows above them are "soft": Even if you paddle straight at them, you will usually be deflected by the pillow and ride off to one side or the other.

Rounded rocks and rocks with blunt upstream faces form pillows readily, whereas those that are pointed on their upstream faces do not form pillows, since the water is quickly carried off to the sides rather than piling up. For this reason, sharp rocks often present more of a pinning hazard than rounded ones, although both can pin you in the right circumstances. Bridge pilings often have sharp upstream faces and can present very bad pinning hazards.

Surf a pillow as you would a hole, by riding up sideways onto it and leaning downstream toward the rock. Brace with your paddle on the rock if necessary. As long as you continue your downstream lean, you will float up on the pillow and be held away from the rock. If you relax your lean and allow the current to grab the upstream edge of your boat, you could find yourself upside down in danger of pinning on the rock.

SEAMS

Two currents meeting at oblique angles form a seam. This can occur when two channels rejoin after splitting around an island or when another river enters from the side. One flow will often fold under the other, making the seam an area of unpredictable current forces.

The most conservative way to deal with a seam is to cross it at right angles with speed. A squirt boater can blast a seam by slicing one end of his boat underwater parallel to the seam and letting the current hold him in a vertical position (see section 2: "Advanced Techniques").

BENDS

As a river goes around a corner, the current on the outside of the bend speeds up due to centrifugal force while that on the inside slows down (fig. 77). The faster current scours the riverbed, making a deeper channel on the outside of the turn and a shallower one on the inside. When maneuvering around bends, keep in mind that the current direction immediately around your boat may not be parallel to the riverbed as shown in figure 77.

RIVER READING

Reading a rapid as you run it is one of the joys of paddling. By tuning in to the water, you lose yourself in keeping up with the constantly changing features. River reading is an essential whitewater skill, since it lets you plan each move rather than paddling blindly down rapids. This way, you choose which rapids you want to run and which you don't, anticipating the effects the current will have on your boat before they occur.

Paddlers give directions on a river as if they were facing downstream. "River right" is the right bank of the river when looking downstream, and "river left" is the left bank of the river when looking downstream.

The best way to learn to read rivers is to be observant when running easy whitewater. Look at the river below you and try to

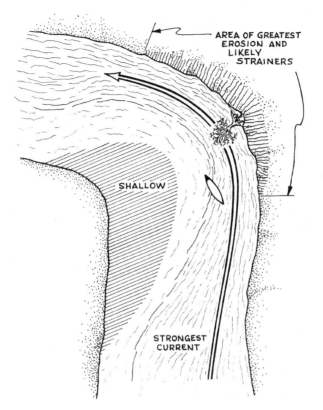

Fig. 77. *A typical river bend showing the faster current on the outside of the turn and the danger of strainers developing where the outside bank is eroded.* Noland Hisey

figure out what each feature tells you about the riverbed. Then as you pass by each feature on your way downstream, look back at it and see if you were correct or not. It also helps to scout rapids from shore, analyzing each feature. Then when you run the rapid, try to pick out the features you saw from shore to see how they look from river level.

The rule of Vs

The rule of Vs is a useful starting point for basic river reading. Vs are formed by the converging (when looking downstream) eddy lines usually found in clear chutes and the diverging eddy lines usually associated with a rock, whether it is out of the

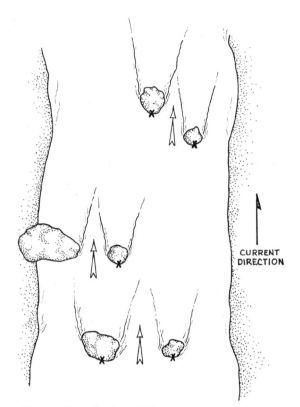

Fig. 78. *The rule of Vs.* Noland Hisey

water or slightly submerged (fig. 78). Downstream-pointing Vs point to clear channels, whereas upstream-pointing Vs point to rocks. Don't use this rule instead of common sense; think of it as a foundation on which to base other river-reading experience.

Scouting

Scouting a rapid means looking ahead to see what you're in for before you get there. It can be done from the boat or from shore. Scouting from the boat is often done by eddy hopping as described under rock gardens (see page 76). But eddy hopping is only reliable if you are very confident of your ability to catch the necessary eddies and if you can see the next good eddy (and enough river between you and it) to be sure there is a clear route.

When the river becomes too steep, obstructed, or large for eddy hopping, you must scout from shore. Pull over, beach your boat, and hike along the riverbank to a vantage point from which you can see the entire rapid, or section of rapid, you are scouting. Some people prefer to scout rapids from downstream to upstream, and some prefer to scout in the opposite direction. Whichever approach you take, begin by identifying significant hazards such as a bad hole, a strainer (see page 187), or an undercut rock (see page 188); This allows you to limit the options to routes that avoid those hazards. Next, choose a route. Depending on your skill level relative to the difficulty of the rapid, you may choose the easiest route, the hardest (or "hero") route, the most playful route, or the one that will leave you the driest. Look for a route that lets you work with the water rather than against it.

Finally, find markers that will tell you where you are in the rapid when you get there. Often what looks like a simple line from shore may be very difficult to follow once it is obscured by rocks, waves, or gradient, all of which may not be apparent from shore. Good markers include a large boulder, a significant tree, a bridge, the third wave, or any other feature that will stand out to you when you are in your boat at river level. Keep an eye on your markers as you walk back to your boat to be sure they'll still be visible from upstream. It often helps to walk to river level and crouch down on shore to get an idea of what the rapid will look like from your boat. In general, rapids are a grade or so harder than they appear from shore. This effect is greatly magnified the higher above a rapid you are when you scout it.

WHITEWATER CLASSIFICATION

Whitewater is classified according to its difficulty and danger from I to VI, with class I water being the easiest, while class VI water is rarely run and presents a very serious risk to life. The international river classification is set out below. Never rely too much on a classification given in a guidebook or by other boaters. In one area of the country, boaters may rate big-water runs a grade harder than average, while boaters in a second region may tend to upgrade technical runs. Your own judgment should always be the ultimate determinant of whether you run a river or not. The classification of a rapid depends on its remoteness, length, water level, and present condition (for example, a strainer that is not there one day may appear the next, making the river more dangerous to run).

International Scale of River Difficulty (from American Whitewater Affiliation Safety Code.)

Class I: Easy. Fast-moving water with riffles and small waves. Few obstructions, all obvious and easily missed with little training. Risk to swimmers is slight; self-rescue is easy (fig. 79).

Class II: Novice. Straightforward rapids with wide, clear channels that are evident without scouting. Occasional maneuvering may be required, but rocks and medium-sized waves are easily avoided by trained paddlers. Swimmers are seldom injured and group assistance, while helpful, is seldom needed (fig. 80).

Class III: Intermediate. Rapids with moderate, irregular waves that may be difficult to avoid and that can swamp an open canoe. Complex maneuvers in fast current and good boat control in tight passages or around ledges are often

Fig. 79. *Typical class I water.* Bruce Lessels

Fig. 80. *Typical class II water.* Bruce Lessels

Fig. 81. *Typical class III water.* Bruce Lessels

required; large waves or strainers may be present but are easily avoided. Strong eddies and powerful current effects can be found, particularly on large-volume rivers. Scouting is advisable for inexperienced parties. Injuries while swimming are rare; self rescue is usually easy but group assistance may be required to avoid long swims (fig. 81).

Fig. 82. *Typical class IV water.* Bruce Lessels

Class IV: Advanced. Intense, powerful, but predictable rapids requiring precise boat handling in turbulent water. Depending on the character of the river, it may feature large, unavoidable waves and holes or constricted passages demanding fast maneuvers under pressure. A fast, reliable eddy turn may be needed to initiate maneuvers, scout rapids, or rest. Rapids may require "must" moves above dangerous hazards. Scouting is necessary the first time down. Risk of injury to swimmers is moderate to high, and water conditions may make self-rescue difficult. Group assistance for rescue is often essential but requires practiced skills. A strong Eskimo roll is highly recommended (fig. 82).

Fig. 83. *Typical class V water.* Jim Gariepy

Class V: Expert. Extremely long, obstructed, or very violent rapids that expose a paddler to above-average danger. Drops may contain large, unavoidable waves and holes or steep, congested chutes with complex, demanding routes. Rapids may continue for long distances between pools, demanding a high level of fitness. What eddies exist may be small, turbulent, or difficult to reach. At the high end of the scale, several of these factors may be combined. Scouting is mandatory but often difficult. Swims are dangerous, and rescue is difficult even for experts. A very reliable Eskimo roll, proper equipment, extensive experience, and practiced rescue skills are essential for survival (fig. 83).

Fig. 84. *Typical class VI water.* Jim Gariepy

Class VI: Extreme. One grade more difficult than class V. These runs exemplify the extremes of difficulty, unpredictability, and danger. The consequences of errors are very severe and rescue may be impossible. For teams of experts only, at favorable water levels, after close personal inspection and taking all precautions. This class does **not** represent drops thought to be unrunnable but may include rapids that are only occasionally run (fig. 84).

Chapter Five

Getting Around on the River

The ability to paddle straight ahead is all that's needed to get down easy rapids. However, this approach quickly becomes hazardous as the difficulty of the water increases. Running straight through large waves, over steep drops, or around sharp corners is like playing Russian roulette on the river, for what lies ahead is never predictable, even from one day to the next.

Upon reading about them, the three basic moves—eddy turns, peelouts, and ferries—may seem solely utilitarian, allowing you to see what's ahead, stop if a boat in your group gets in trouble, or get from one side of the river to the other. Once mastered, however, they become ends in themselves. Every beginner paddler who has done even one well-executed eddy turn or precisely angled ferry knows the satisfaction of working with and getting to know the river rather than making a beeline for the bottom of each rapid.

LEANING IN CURRENT

Many beginners have a natural aversion to being sideways in the current. But to perform whitewater moves, you must be comfortable at any angle. To avoid the unstable feeling that comes with being sideways, you must learn to lean correctly. The general rules to remember are: When in the main current, always lean downstream; and when entering or leaving an eddy, always lean into the turn. If you get into squirt boating or racing, you'll have to relearn some of this, but for beginning whitewater paddling the simple rules apply.

To understand why the first rule works, think of sitting in your boat on a rug and having it pulled out from under you. Your boat will tend to roll away from the direction in which the rug is being pulled, or, substituting the river for the rug, your boat will tend to roll upstream. You counteract this tendency by leaning downstream. If the rug you are sitting on is moving, and you are staying stationary on it, your boat won't tend to flip one way or the other.

The second rule, to always lean into the turn, is easy to understand intuitively if you think of riding a bicycle. When you're turning into or out of an eddy, your boat crosses from current moving downstream to current moving upstream. You lean into the turn in order to counteract the rug-pulling effect of the current you are entering.

Ideally, all your leans on whitewater should be j leans to maintain the isolation of your upper and lower body so your paddle can act independently from your boat. In reality, however, no one always leans correctly, which is why bracing and rolling are important whitewater skills.

Correct lean is critical when you are about to float sideways, or broach, on a rock. Intuition tells you to lean away (or upstream) from the rock. By leaning upstream and away from the rock, you will find yourself instantly in the water and possibly pinned up against the rock. If instead, you lean toward the rock (as shown in fig. 85), you will avoid flipping and can take your time working your way off it.

Fig. 85. *Leaning toward a rock will prevent you from flipping and give you time to work your way off it.* Karen Blom

EDDY TURNS AND PEELOUTS

The calm water in an eddy provides a resting spot on the river. It is a place to regroup; to stop and scout the rapid ahead; or from which to surf waves, holes, or initiate a series of moves. If for no other reason, the joy of executing eddy turns and peelouts is reason enough to learn and practice them.

Eddy Turns

Enter an eddy using an eddy turn, and leave it with a peelout. Both moves use the current differential between the eddy water and the main current to turn the boat. An eddy turn consists of the following parts (fig. 86):

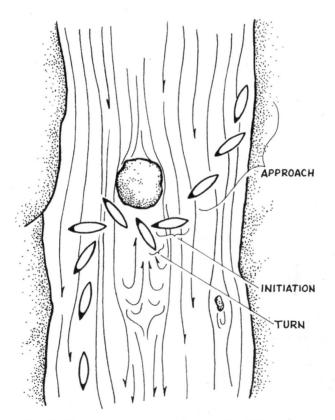

Fig. 86. *The three phases of an eddy turn.* John Urban

1. The approach, during which you set an angle with your boat toward the eddy and drive across the current toward the eddy line.
2. The initiation, which starts you turning into the eddy as your boat crosses the eddy line.
3. The turn, where you use your paddle as a pivot point and, taking advantage of the different current forces on your boat, swing around into the eddy, finally coming to rest with your bow pointing directly upstream.

The approach is the most important part of an eddy turn, since most of the turning itself is done by the river. An ideal approach has you crossing the eddy line a few feet below the rock, at about seventy to ninety degrees to the eddy line with a good deal of cross-current momentum (fig. 87). In order to accomplish this, start to set up early—fifty to several hundred feet upstream of the eddy. To account for the downstream movement of the river, aim for a point higher in the eddy than where you want eventually to end.

The eddy is strongest just below the rock, so coming in high helps you make maximum use of the eddy/current differential. Pointing your bow right at the rock usually gives you enough

Fig. 87. *The approach. Note the boat is perpendicular to the current and aiming at the rock.* Karen Blom

leeway to hit the eddy high after accounting for the river's downstream movement. If you never hit the rock in an eddy turn, you're not entering high enough.

Don't be shy about angling your boat across the river. The more perpendicular to the current your boat is when it crosses the eddy line, the less turning it has to do in the eddy. It is also easier to convert the momentum gained on the approach to upstream momentum in the eddy if you approach from the side rather than from directly upstream. However, going past ninety degrees so your bow is starting to point upstream before hitting the eddy line will often cause you to get stuck on the eddy line rather than to penetrate it. While it is possible to ferry into most eddies, it is generally easier to cross an eddy line at right angles.

Once you have pointed your boat at the eddy, take a few strokes forward to get your boat moving toward it. Solo canoeists should not hesitate to do cross forward strokes in this situation, even if they are on the upstream side of the boat, since it is crucial to pick up momentum in order to cross the current efficiently. Don't forget to lean slightly downstream as you do this, since your boat should be moving sideways in the river, bringing the rug-pulling effect into play.

Once your bow is at the eddy line, you are ready to start the turn. There are two possible initiation strokes. The first is a forward sweep on the downstream side for a kayaker or a canoeist with his paddle on the downstream side as shown in figures 88 and 89. The second is an overcorrection on the upstream side for a canoeist with his paddle on the upstream side. To overcorrect, hold a j stroke or pry a little longer than necessary so that it starts to turn the boat toward your on side. A solo paddler with his paddle upstream may also use a cross forward sweep to initiate an eddy turn, but this can be unstable, since the cross forward sweep comes while he is shifting his lean from one side to the other.

Shift your lean into the turn just as you cross the eddy line. This can be tricky, since it is often difficult to distinguish exactly where the eddy line starts and ends, but generally as you finish your sweep, you should have completed your lean into the eddy.

The turn happens by itself if you've approached and initiated well. The two remaining tasks are to provide a pivot stroke

Figs. 88 and 89. *The initiation using a forward sweep. (Side view and top view in a kayak and C-1.)* Karen Blom

Fig. 89. Bruce Lessels

to guide the boat into the eddy and to maintain the correct lean. The pivot stroke you choose depends on your experience, the turbulence of the eddy, and your own preference, but there are four possibilities: a duffek (fig. 90) or cross draw (fig. 91), a high brace (fig. 92), or a low brace.

Fig. 90. *The turn using a duffek in a kayak.* Karen Blom

Fig. 91. *The turn using a cross draw in an off-side C-1.* Bruce Lessels

Fig. 92. *A high brace being used as the pivot stroke on an eddy turn.* Karen Blom

Whichever stroke you use for the pivot, it should be done on the inside of the turn or the opposite side of the boat from the initiation stroke (unless the initiation stroke was an overcorrection on the upstream side of the boat). The pivot stroke is static: Plant your blade in the eddy water and let the centrifugal force of the turn and the upstream current in the eddy lock it in place while your boat spins around it. A duffek is the most aggressive pivot stroke, since it gives you a pivot point as well as a rudder with which to vary the tightness of the turn. You can easily convert a duffek to a forward stroke to finish the eddy turn and maintain your position in the eddy. The disadvantage of a duffek is that it will not support your weight as a brace would, so to use a duffek in an eddy, you must be confident that your j lean will be steady enough to keep you from capsizing. The high brace is the next most aggressive stroke for entering an eddy. While it does not provide the directional control of a duffek, it offers support as you enter the eddy. The high brace can also be feathered forward into a forward stroke to finish the eddy turn in a similar fashion to the duffek. The low brace, because it uses the back face of the blade, is a very stable way of entering an eddy but gives virtually no directional control and does not convert easily into a forward stroke.

No matter how you enter an eddy, you will often find that upon completing the turn you are facing upstream but still moving slowly downstream out of the eddy. Paddle forward to complete the maneuver and keep yourself solidly in the eddy. This is where being able to convert your pivot stroke to a forward stroke is useful.

Coordinating an eddy turn in a tandem canoe. In a tandem canoe, setting the angle of approach and the general line into the eddy is the job of the stern paddler. The bow paddler's job during the approach is to provide power and help to set the angle if the stern paddler is having difficulty.

The stern paddler is responsible for the initiation stroke, which will be either a forward sweep/stern draw or an overcorrection using the j stroke or pry. The bow paddler does the pivot stroke (figs. 93 and 94) and is responsible for the timing of the turn. He decides when to give the boat a solid pivot point by planting his paddle in the eddy water. Once the bow paddler has planted his pivot stroke, the stern paddler continues a forward sweep or converts his extended correction stroke into a reverse sweep depending on his paddling side.

Fig. 93. *The bow paddler does the pivot stroke in a tandem boat. In this on-side eddy turn, the bow paddler is using a duffek.* Karen Blom

Fig. 94. *This eddy turn is to the bow paddler's off side, so he is using a cross draw as the pivot stroke.* Noland Hisey

Peelouts

Peelouts work in much the same way as eddy turns. From your position in the eddy, drive upstream at the top of the eddy line, pointing your bow at about eleven o'clock or one o'clock (pointing right at the rock would be twelve o'clock). Your last stroke in the eddy should be a sweep on the upstream side (fig. 95) for

Fig. 95. *A sweep on the upstream side used to initiate a peelout.* Bruce Lessels

kayakers and off-side canoeists or an extended correction stroke on the downstream side for on-side canoeists. Your next stroke should be a pivot stroke in the current— either a duffek (fig. 96), high brace (fig. 97), or low brace (fig. 98)—the trade-offs are the same as those described above for eddy turns. In a tandem canoe the bow paddler will be the one to execute this stroke while the stern paddler continues his sweep or converts his

Fig. 96. *A duffek used to leave an eddy in a kayak.* Jobeth Hager

Fig. 97. *A cross high brace used to peel out of an eddy in a tandem canoe.* Karen Blom

Fig. 98. *A low brace/reverse sweep being used to leave an eddy in a tandem canoe.* Bruce Lessels

extended correction into a reverse sweep. Remember to lean downstream as the bow crosses the eddy line.

Two common mistakes in peelouts are to leave the eddy with too little speed to cross the eddy line cleanly and to leave with an angle that is too perpendicular to the current you are entering, which causes your bow to swing downstream early and may land you on the eddy line rather than sending you smoothly out into the river.

When peeling out into a wave train, you can speed your peelout by putting your bow on the downstream face of a wave as it enters the current. This will cause your bow to fall down the wave as it peels out, adding the force of gravity to that of the current pulling you downstream. Conversely, you can peel out onto the upstream face of a wave to widen your turn.

S turns

Combining eddy turns and peelouts into s turns is a great way to practice these maneuvers. There are two types of s turns, both of which require you to use a duffek on the eddy turn and the peelout to experience the full effect of the maneuver.

In the first type of s turn, you enter an eddy from one side and immediately after entering it, peel out on the opposite side (fig. 99). The trick is to carry your momentum through the entire turn by converting the duffek you use to enter the eddy into a sweep that will be used to exit the eddy before your boat is completely facing upstream. This maneuver is fluid and exciting and can be useful when you need to work your way across the river.

To do the second type of s turn, peel out of one eddy and immediately enter an eddy on the opposite side of the river (fig. 100). The duffek used on your peelout can also be converted into a sweep as in the first s turn. If the eddies are close enough together, the entire maneuver can be done on one continuous stroke.

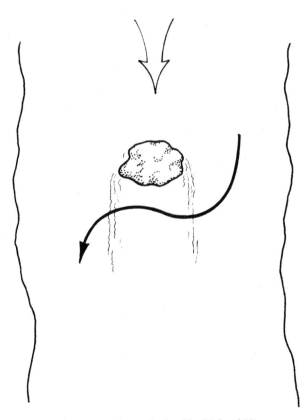

Fig. 99. *An s turn using a single eddy.* Noland Hisey

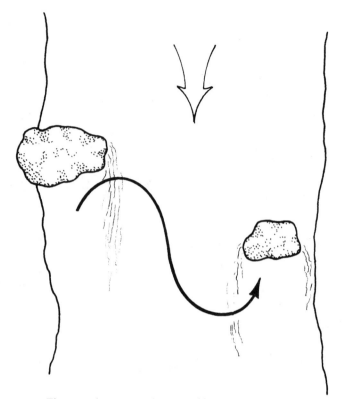

Fig. 100. *An s turn using two eddies.* Noland Hisey

FERRIES

Ferrying allows you to move from one side of the river to the other without being pulled downstream by the current. In ferrying you paddle at an angle to the river, presenting one side of the boat or the other to the current (fig. 101). If you angle your boat slightly toward one shore, the current will push on the upstream side of it, moving you toward that shore as you paddle against the current. The more angle you use, the faster your ferry will be, but also the more you risk being turned completely broadside by the current and swept downstream. If you have too little angle, you will spend all your energy fighting the current rather than using it to send you across the river.

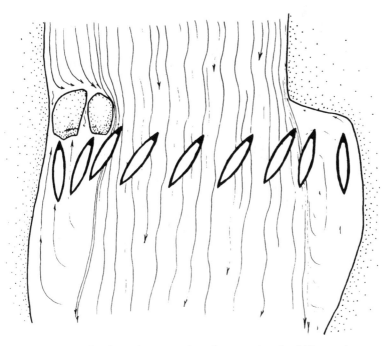

Fig. 101. *Ferrying by setting an angle to the current and paddling upstream allows you to cross a river without losing ground.* John Urban

Ferries usually start from eddies, although you can also initiate a ferry simply by turning upstream in midriver and starting to paddle against the current at an angle. When ferrying from an eddy, your first concern is the angle of the boat as it enters the current. The more parallel to the current your boat is (a conservative angle), the more easily you will be able to control its angle as it enters the current. The more perpendicular to the current it is (a radical angle), the more the current will tend to sweep your bow downstream the moment it crosses the eddy line.

You must also have adequate speed as your boat crosses the eddy line. This allows you to spend as little time as possible on this no-man's-land where the current wants to make your boat peel out rather than allow your bow to remain pointing upstream in a ferry angle. It often helps to back up a few strokes in the eddy to allow yourself room to pick up speed. Pushing off a rock with your paddle also works well for canoeists (fig. 102).

Fig. 102. *Pushing off a rock can help you gain speed quickly in tight spots. The rock the paddler is using is just below the surface.* Karen Blom

As you cross the eddy line, lean downstream using a j lean, and be ready to do a correcting stroke to maintain your angle. This can be either a forward sweep on the downstream side for kayakers and on-side canoeists (fig. 103), or a pry or cross forward sweep for off-side canoeists. In a tandem canoe, the stern paddler sets and maintains the angle using either a forward sweep, when his paddle is on the downstream side (fig. 104), or a pry when his paddle is on the upstream side (fig. 105). The bow paddler provides the power but can do little to help with the angle.

Once out in the current, maintain your angle with sweeps, pries, and rudders. Experiment with more radical and conservative angles to vary the speed of your ferry. Try to do as much forward paddling as possible to neutralize the current. Don't get too caught up with correction strokes.

You can often take advantage of a wave to help you ferry. Place your bow in the trough as you leave the eddy and take a stroke on the downstream side of your boat on top of the wave.

Fig. 103. *Crossing the eddy line on a ferry. Note the powerful forward sweep on the downstream side and the downstream lean.* Bruce Lessels

Fig. 104. *The stern paddler maintains the angle in a tandem boat. In this case he is using a forward sweep.* Noland Hisey

Fig 105. *Using a pry to maintain boat angle when beginning an off-side ferry in a canoe.* Noland Hisey

A ferry usually ends as you cross into the eddy on the opposite side of the river from your starting eddy. Crossing the eddy line can be difficult. It will try to turn your boat upstream, leaving you stuck halfway between the current and the eddy. To avoid this, increase your ferry angle (making it more radical) for the final stroke in the current before you hit the eddy line. Increase the angle by sweeping on the upstream side or doing a quick pry on the downstream side while leaning back to unweight your bow. Lightening the bow helps it get over the eddy line without being grabbed by the eddy water right away. This allows you to penetrate the eddy line as you do during an eddy turn. As you cross the eddy line, don't forget to shift your lean from downstream to into the eddy turn.

Back Ferries

In most ferries, your bow is pointed upstream, since you can neutralize the current more effectively paddling forward than backward. However, there are some situations in which a ferry with your bow pointed downstream is useful or fun. Back ferries allow you to move from side to side above an unknown drop to see what might be downstream. They are sometimes helpful when quick maneuvering is needed but there is not enough time to spin your boat and paddle forward to avoid an obstacle. Open boaters carrying heavy gear often back ferry to get around sharp bends without being swept into the outside bank or to go through heavy wave trains without taking on water.

The theory is exactly the same as that for upstream ferries described above. Cross the eddy line at a conservative angle with sufficient speed. The trick is to steer the boat effectively while paddling backward. It helps to use compound back strokes in a canoe or to look over the current-side shoulder in a kayak.

As you cross the eddy line, lean downstream and be prepared to maintain your angle with a reverse sweep or cross back stroke (in a solo canoe) on the downstream side. Once in the current, correct your angle using reverse sweeps or bow pries (for off-side canoeists). The bow paddler controls the angle in a back ferry in a tandem canoe using reverse sweeps and bow pries.

SURFING WAVES AND HOLES

Wave surfing

Surfing a river wave is similar to surfing an ocean wave, but on rivers the waves stay in the same place, making it theoretically possible to surf one forever. To ride a wave, you must make the force of gravity that is pulling you down into the upstream trough of the wave equal the force of the current that is pushing you downstream so you stay in one place in the middle of the river. Surfing is an efficient way to move from one side of the river to the other, and the feeling of riding a wave with the river rushing by you is one of the ultimate thrills in whitewater (fig. 106)!

To learn to surf, find a smooth, low-angle wave about one to three feet high with a good eddy next to it and a safe runout below it. Get onto the wave by ferrying out of the eddy so that as you cross the eddy line your bow lands in the trough of the wave. As soon as your boat is across the eddy line, use a pry on the upstream side or a forward sweep on the downstream side to kill your ferry angle and bring you parallel to the current (fig. 107).

Fig. 106. *Surfing a river wave.* Bruce Lessels

Fig. 107. *Once out in the current, use forward sweeps or pries to bring the boat parallel to the current.* Karen Blom

If you time it right, you will end up facing upstream with your body just upstream of the peak of the wave you are surfing and your bow down in the trough as in figure 107. If your bow starts to bury in the trough of the wave, lean back to keep your weight toward the stern, and lean your boat up on edge to allow the bow to slice up out of the water. If your bow is still burying, you may need to cut back and forth to maintain your position on the wave.

To cut back and forth, or "shred" a wave, set a ferry angle in one direction and allow your boat to shoot across the wave toward one shore. Before falling off the wave or entering the eddy on the other side, change your angle to ferry back in the other direction by using either a pry or rudder on the upstream side or a forward sweep on the downstream side of your boat. When you change your ferry angle, quickly shift your lean, since by cutting (changing your angle) you have changed the downstream edge of your boat from one side to the other. Use only j leans in order to keep your paddle free to control the boat's angle.

You can make these cuts as quick as you want depending on the size and shape of the wave. The steeper the wave you surf and the longer the boat you're paddling, the more often you will need to cut. In general, shorter boats with lower-volume sterns are easier to surf than are longer, more rounded boats.

The approach you use to get onto a wave is very important. Many boaters try to overshoot a wave by entering the current upstream of it, expecting to float downstream toward the wave, then kill their momentum the instant they get to it. The problem with this approach is that with difficult surfing waves you may have too much downstream momentum by the time you hit the wave, and no amount of paddling can neutralize the current enough to get you surfing. A better approach is to enter the current with your bow in the correct position and with sufficient momentum to end up right in the trough of the wave once you have ferried across the eddy line. This way you should be able to carry the momentum you have generated in the eddy onto the wave and have the current speed neutralize the momentum just as you come into a surfing position. While this approach takes more experience and better judgment of the current speed and direction, it saves you considerable work.

Back surfing

Back surfing tests your feel for the current. While the principle is the same as forward surfing, the mechanics are less intuitive. Back paddling out of the eddy next to the wave you want to surf, lean forward to keep your stern from burying in the trough, and use a reverse sweep or cross back stroke on the downstream side to maintain your angle. Once you are on the wave, kill your angle with a reverse sweep or cross back stroke. Maintain your angle using reverse sweeps, bow pries, and cross back strokes. Oh, and don't forget to lean downstream!

Hole surfing

Holes can be intimidating when you understand the forces involved. Some are indeed dangerous, but small- to medium-sized holes are often fun to surf. Learning to ride holes is important for paddling in difficult rapids. Inadvertent hole surfing is an inevitable part of class III and above paddling.

When you surf a hole, the current on the surface that recirculates from below opposes the current coming over the ledge that forms the hole. Your boat is held between the two in equilibrium (fig. 108). The first thing to think about is lean—it should be downstream, and it must be solid. Any variation in your lean that allows the current coming over the ledge to grab the upstream edge of your boat results in a quick upstream flip known as "window shading."

Fig. 108. *Hole surfing.* Bruce Lessels

Fig. 109. *Leaning in balance in a hole.* Karen Blom

You may need to use your paddle for partial support, but try to lean in balance when possible to keep your paddle free so you can power out of the hole when you want to. When you first enter a hole, you will usually need a high or low brace until you are stable and have figured out the correct lean. Once stable, experiment with taking your paddle out of the water for short periods to develop a consistent in-balance lean (fig. 109). Be careful to keep your elbows low when doing either a high or low brace, since the powerful jerking motions of hole surfing can easily cause shoulder dislocations.

Escaping from a hole. You can exit a hole in several ways: by paddling out either end, by Eskimo rolling, or by endering out. Paddling out either end is the easiest and most common method of exiting a hole. Of course this only works if at least one end is unobstructed. To use this method, take as much weight as possible off your paddle and paddle forward or back, working your way to the open end (fig. 110). In steep holes, these strokes may have to be interspersed with braces to maintain your balance, or you may have to use a hybrid stroke where you put your paddle in the water at forty-five degrees to the current and do a combination high brace–forward stroke. If

Fig. 110. *Taking a forward stroke to exit from a hole.* Karen Blom

your first attempt does not work, back up and try again, using the momentum gained from rocking back and forth to build speed out the open end.

To roll out of a hole, simply flip upside down, wait a short time until you feel yourself clear the hole, and roll back up. This is not necessarily as easy as it sounds and does not work in larger holes, but in holes with shallow recycles, it allows your body, when hanging underwater, to grab the deep current moving downstream that will often pull the boat over the recycle and out. If this is not working, you may want to try to actively grab the deep water with your paddle while upside down. (See chapter 6 for more on rolling techniques.)

A final technique, although more advanced than the other two, is to try to ender or back ender out of a hole. Enders are described under advanced techniques, but the idea is to try to paddle out one end of the hole until your boat is more or less parallel to the current with one end facing back up into the hole, and then let that end of your boat dive into the trough causing you to do an ender and be thrown clear. This is generally used in large, serious holes and is not a beginner technique.

Chapter Six

Eskimo Rolling

One of the most rewarding moves in paddling is the Eskimo roll in which a canoe or kayak is brought back upright after a capsize. By allowing you to recover from an upset, rolling extends your comfort range on whitewater tremendously and makes you a safer paddler. A paddler who is confident of his roll can play in the midst of a difficult rapid knowing it's likely he can recover quickly and easily if he flips.

Contrary to popular opinion, there is no magic to rolling. The motions are relatively simple: A strong "hip snap" rights the boat, while the paddle blade, which is placed flat on the water, acts as a support. The environment in which rolling takes place can make it difficult to learn if you are not completely comfortable upside down underwater. The best way to deal with this fear is to practice your roll again and again in a pond or pool until it becomes second nature.

Kayakers, closed canoeists, and open canoeists can all roll with proper outfitting. If possible, learn with the help of an experienced paddler. This "coach" can not only critique you but can also provide the physical support needed to practice the movements of a roll. Everyone learns to roll at his or her own pace, and every individual has his or her own particular rough spots. A good coach can identify these spots and assist in overcoming them.

Of course everyone misses their roll once in a while, so a reliable roll does not obviate the need for additional safety measures. It simply makes them necessary less often.

ESKIMO RESCUE

The Eskimo rescue can lessen the amount of swimming you do while learning to roll. It allows one boater to help another by

111

extending the bow of his boat to the capsized paddler. As soon as the capsized paddler has determined he is not going to roll, he should let go of his paddle and start to slide his hands along the sides of his boat to let other paddlers know he is looking for an Eskimo rescue (fig. 111), and to search for the bow of another paddler's boat. The rescuing paddler then paddles at the capsized paddler, prodding the upside-down boat gently with his

Fig. 111. *Setting up for an Eskimo rescue.* Karen Blom

Fig. 112. *Rolling up off another boater's bow.* Karen Blom

bow to let the capsized paddler know he is there. As soon as the capsized paddler feels and can grab the rescuer's boat, he uses its bow to roll up as shown in figure 112.

The Eskimo rescue works well in flatwater and easy whitewater when all paddlers in a group are aware it will be used, so they can keep a close watch on each other and react quickly to a capsize. It should not be done on rapids with obvious hazards at the bottom, since the paddler underwater cannot see where he is heading and, therefore, cannot react to hazards. The capsized paddler attempting an Eskimo rescue should know his own limits and only wait for as long as he feels comfortable underwater, allowing some extra air to give him time to exit and swim to the surface. If he feels himself hitting the bottom, or is at all uncertain of the situation downstream, he should exit right away.

CANOE ROLLS

On-side roll

The most common canoe roll is actually just a very deep low brace. It is sometimes difficult to get to a low-brace position from underwater, however, since being upside down can be disorienting. Rolling to your on side is the easiest and most powerful way to right a canoe after a capsize.

The on-side roll can be broken into three phases: the setup, the sweep, and the brace up.

In the setup, you tuck forward on the deck of your boat to protect your face and body from underwater rocks. Line your paddle up along your off-side seam line or gunwale in front of you with the blade end pointing forward and the power face facing up (fig. 113). Maintain this position as you flip over until you are totally upside down (fig. 114).

The sweep begins by moving the paddle in an arc out to the side on which it was set up (figs. 115 and 116). Keep your bottom arm straight throughout the sweep, and stretch for the water's surface with your head and your bottom hand. At the end of the sweep your paddle shaft should be perpendicular to the boat, and your head and shoulders should be just under the surface of the water. Ideally, you should be able to feel air on the knuckles of your lower hand (the paddle blade should be on or above the water's surface).

Fig. 113. *The setup position for a canoe roll demonstrated in a covered canoe , or C-1.* Karen Blom

Fig. 114. *Remaining in the setup position until you are totally upside down protects your head and upper body.* Karen Blom

Fig. 115. *The beginning of the sweep seen from above water. Note the paddle is on or above the surface of the water.* Karen Blom

Fig. 116. *At the end of the sweep, the paddle is at ninety degrees to the boat and still on or near the surface.* Karen Blom

Fig. 117. *Flipping the paddle over to use the non–power face of the blade.*
Karen Blom

Fig. 118. *Beginning to low brace up as seen from underwater.*
Karen Blom

To finish the roll, brace up by flipping your paddle over so you are using the non–power face of the blade (fig. 117) and doing a low brace (figs. 118 and 119). You flip the paddle by rotating both wrists forward and at the same time turning your torso so you are looking at the bottom of the river. Then, keeping your head on the surface of the water (your face is still in the water), pull on your on-side knee and push on your off-side knee while driving your head down with the paddle (fig. 120).

Common mistakes are bringing your head up too soon in an attempt to breathe before the boat is upright; not starting with your paddle on the surface of the water; failing to tuck forward on the way over; and relying too much on the paddle for support, rather than developing a strong hip snap to right the boat.

Fig. 119. *Beginning to low brace up as seen from above water.* Karen Blom

Fig. 120. *Finishing a C-1 roll. Note that the boat is almost upright again, but the head is still in the water.* Karen Blom

High brace roll

A canoe can be rolled using a high brace, although this roll is not as powerful as the low brace roll. To do the high brace roll, follow the steps described above, but don't flip the blade over just before bracing up. This is essentially a kayak C-to-C roll (see next section) done in a canoe. This roll can be very hard on your shoulders.

Off-side roll

To roll to your off side takes considerably more flexibility than an on-side roll. Some paddlers prefer to switch hands rather than rolling off-side. However you do it, developing an effective roll on both sides of the boat is the best insurance against unnecessary swims.

An off-side roll can be broken down into the same three phases as the on-side roll. The setup is similar to the on-side setup except that the paddle should be placed along the centerline of the bow deck (fig. 121). The blade end again points toward the bow, and the power face is up.

Fig. 121. *Setting up for an off-side roll in a C-1.* Karen Blom

Once upside down, move the paddle into position by rotating your torso so it faces toward your on side and sweeping the paddle out at ninety degrees to the boat on your on side (fig. 122). Again, you should feel air on the knuckles of your bottom hand, and your head should be close to the surface of the water.

Fig. 122. *Sweeping the paddle out at ninety degrees toward your on side.* Karen Blom

To complete the roll, brace up by flipping your paddle over so you are using the non–power face (fig. 123). This is done by rotating both wrists back. Now pull on your off-side knee and

Fig. 123. *Flipping the paddle over so you are rolling using the non–power face of the blade.* Karen Blom

Fig. 124. *Completing an off-side C-1 roll.* Karen Blom

push on your on-side knee while driving down with your head and the paddle (fig. 124). Again, your head should come out of the water last.

Unless you are extremely flexible, you may find it difficult to break this roll into distinct sweep and brace-up phases. This breakdown is presented here simply to help you think about the roll.

Reverse sweep roll

This is a specialized roll that is very helpful when properly used but can be dangerous in the wrong circumstances since it exposes your face. The time to use this roll is when you flip surfing a wave or coming off an ender. In both situations, you generally go over with your body on the back deck of the boat, and the water you land in is usually deep. The reverse sweep roll allows you to right yourself immediately from this position rather than tucking all the way forward and doing a standard low brace roll. This roll also uses a low brace, and many of the principles are the same as the standard on-side roll described above.

To start a reverse sweep roll, lean back onto the stern deck of your boat with your paddle blade pointing toward the stern and your t grip in front of your face (fig. 125). The palm of your

Fig. 125. *Setting up for a reverse sweep roll in a C-1. This position leaves your face and upper body exposed, so it should only be used in places that are known to be deep.* Karen Blom

Fig. 126. *Sweeping the entire upper body and paddle toward the off side in a reverse sweep roll.* Karen Blom

Fig. 127. *Bracing up in a reverse sweep roll.* Karen Blom

t-grip hand should be toward your face. Now flip to your off side. Once underwater, sweep your entire upper body and paddle together out to your off side (fig. 126), then rotate your torso so you are looking at the bottom of the river, and drive down with your head and paddle while pulling on your on-side knee and pushing on your off-side knee (fig. 127).

The key to this roll is that your upper body and paddle must move together. The relationship between your upper body and your paddle determined in the setup position described above should be maintained throughout the roll. A reverse sweep roll can also be done to your off side by sweeping out to the opposite side with your body and paddle after flipping over.

Special considerations for open-canoe rolling

The most important factor in open-canoe rolling is proper outfitting. The more air bags you have in your boat, the easier it will be to roll. Snug outfitting is a must. Hip pads make you slip around in the boat less, and tight thigh straps help hold your knees on the knee pads.

Boat design is also a factor in rolling an open canoe. The wider the boat, the more difficult it will be to roll, since width makes it more stable both right-side up and upside down. It is also difficult to reach far enough out from the gunwales with your paddle to roll a wide boat effectively. Boats with extreme rocker can also be difficult to roll, since the ends tend to hit the water first and prevent the boat from flipping all the way over. Even when upside down, highly rockered boats can be difficult to roll, because your lower body is hanging much farther out of the water than in less-rockered designs.

When recovering from an open-canoe roll be sure to keep your head low, bringing it across the boat just above the gunwales at the last minute. Be sure your head is past the centerline of the boat before ending the roll (figs. 128 through 131).

Fig. 128. *Rolling an open canoe is not as difficult as it sounds. Be sure your head is past the centerline of the boat (fig. 131) before sitting up.* Susan Connolly

Fig. 129. Susan Connolly

Fig. 130. Susan Connolly

Fig. 131. Susan Connolly

Coordinating a C-2 (tandem canoe) roll

To roll with a partner you need to work out a system to coordinate your efforts. Several systems work. You should pick the one that fits your paddling style and preference.

First, decide on which side you will roll. Seeing a C-2 come straight out of the water, then settle back down again as the two paddlers try to roll on opposite sides, is one of the great comic sights in whitewater for the spectators but sure cause for friction between the partners. Whichever side you decide to roll on, one partner must either switch hands or do an off-side roll.

The partner that switches or rolls off-side is usually slower to start than the other, so he should be the one to signal when he is ready to roll. There are two types of signals he can use. The movement of the roll itself can be a signal—when the other partner feels the first start to roll, he kicks in his own roll—or the initiating partner can hit the boat with his paddle producing an audible signal as well as a vibration in the boat that can be heard or felt by his partner.

KAYAK ROLLS

C-to-C roll

The most commonly taught kayak roll is the C-to-C roll. This is due in part to the ease with which it can be taught and in part to the protected position it leaves you in at the end. The C-to-C roll is named for the motion your upper body goes through. Your torso moves from curving to one side to form a C to curving to the other side to form a mirror-image C.

This roll can be broken down in the same fashion as the canoe roll: the setup, sweep, and brace up.

To set up, tuck your head forward on the deck and line your paddle up along the seam line on the nonactive side, the side away from the side on which you are going to come up (fig. 132). The power face of the active blade should be facing up, which may require you to cock the active wrist forward. As you flip over, be sure to maintain the setup position (figs. 133 and 134). Don't relax your back or arms, since this tends to pull your paddle underwater when you are upside down.

Once you are completely over, sweep your paddle out to the side on which it is set up (fig. 135). Your nonactive arm and

Fig. 132. *Setup position for the C-to-C roll in a kayak.* Karen Blom

Fig. 133. *Maintain the setup position when upside down.* Karen Blom

blade need to go up over the hull of the boat. This allows your active blade to sweep out to a right angle. In this position, you should be able to feel air on the knuckles of your active hand, and your nonactive elbow should be touching the bottom of the boat. Your torso should form its first C with the edge of the cockpit rim hitting your ribs on your nonactive side.

Fig. 134. Karen Blom

Fig. 135. *At the end of the sweep phase of a C-to-C roll, your paddle should be perpendicular to the boat and on the surface of the water.* Karen Blom

Brace up by moving your body from the first C position (fig. 136) to the second (fig. 137). This movement is done with your entire upper body from your hips to your head. In the first C position your spine should form a C toward your nonactive side when viewed from the front, while in the second C posi-

Fig. 136. *The third phase of the C-to-C roll is bracing up by moving your torso from one C position (fig. 136) to the other (fig. 137).* Karen Blom

Fig. 137. Karen Blom

tion, it should form a C toward your active side when viewed from the front. Hold your elbows in close to your body. Extending your nonactive arm much at this point can cause shoulder dislocations and cause your active blade to form a more vertical angle to the surface of the water, lessening its ability to support your weight.

Perfecting the C-to-C motion with your torso and hips is very important before trying to add the paddle motion and putting it all together. Practice with a helper standing in the water or by using a dock, swimming pool side, or other boat as a support. To put the motions together, it helps to practice them on shore before trying them in the water.

Once you are comfortable with the hip motion (the C-to-C) and have practiced the three phases of the roll on shore with the paddle, try flipping over and having a helper move your paddle through the three positions while you are underwater. Do the C-to-C motion after the helper has taken you through the sweep phase, and try to build your muscles' memory of the paddle movements as the helper is positioning your paddle. Use the helper's support less and less until you are rolling on your own.

Sweep roll

If you lack the flexibility to do a C-to-C roll, the sweep roll is an effective alternative. The sweep roll has only two distinguishable phases: the setup and the sweep. You brace up throughout the sweep phase.

The setup on the sweep roll is virtually identical to that for the C-to-C roll. The only difference is that on setting up for a sweep roll, it is important to angle your active blade slightly so it will climb across the surface of the water as you are sweeping. This means you have to cock your wrists slightly more for a sweep roll than for a C-to-C.

Once you are upside down, sweep your paddle out to the side on which it is set up, maintaining the climbing angle on your active blade (fig. 138). The hip motion should start just after the sweep begins. The sweep continues toward the stern (fig. 139) until your head finally comes out of the water on the stern deck (fig. 140). Finishing the roll in this exposed position is one disadvantage of the sweep roll. Throughout the sweep, be certain to keep both elbows in close to your body as in the C-to-C roll to minimize the danger of dislocation and to maintain a horizontal paddle angle on the surface of the water.

Fig. 138. *Maintaining a climbing angle on the active blade is essential during a sweep roll.* Karen Blom

Fig. 139. *Sweep toward the stern while righting the boat with your hips at the same time.* Karen Blom

Fig. 140. *The end of a sweep showing the head recovering in a relatively exposed position toward the rear deck.* Karen Blom

Extended paddle roll

In this roll you change the position of your hands on the paddle, giving you a "longer" paddle to use. Some people find the extended paddle roll easier to learn at first, since it helps them gain leverage with the paddle and allows them to orient the blade more easily than a roll using the standard grip. However, it is not effective for advanced paddlers because the setup is so slow. Both the sweep roll and the C-to-C roll can be done with an extended paddle.

To do either a sweep or a C-to-C roll with an extended paddle, choke up with your grip on the shaft during the setup, extending your paddle forward when it is on the seam line so that your nonactive hand grasps the nonactive blade (fig. 141). By holding the blade this way, you are sure to have the correct angle on the other blade if your paddle has an offset around ninety degrees. With offsets of much less than ninety degrees, you may have to adjust the angle of the nonactive blade to achieve a climbing angle on the active blade. The rest of the roll remains the same.

Reverse sweep roll

This roll can be used in kayak as well as canoe, although it is awkward because the nonactive blade gets in the way. It is

Fig. 141. *The setup for an extended paddle roll.* David Eden

sometimes useful for recovering from a flip while surfing a wave or after doing an ender. However, it exposes your face, so it is only safe to do in deep water.

Set up by leaning back on the rear deck and holding your paddle so the active blade points toward the stern (fig. 142). The shaft should be right in front of your face, and the non–power

Fig. 142. *Setting up for the reverse sweep roll in a kayak.* Bruce Lessels

Fig. 143. *The end of a reverse sweep roll. Note paddle is in low-brace position.* Karen Blom

face of the active blade should face up. After flipping in this position, sweep your torso and paddle as a unit forward and toward your nonactive side to right your boat in a low brace (fig. 143). This low brace roll may feel awkward at first in a kayak, since your boat interferes with the nonactive blade, keeping your active blade from being as flat on the water as would be ideal.

HAND ROLL

To prove it's all in the hips, try rolling using only your hands (fig. 144). There are times when this comes in handy on a river, such as when you drop or break your paddle on the way over, or when the crowds on shore are asking for a show. Learning to hand roll also improves your hip snap and will inevitably sharpen your paddle roll.

The rolls described above in both kayak and canoe can be done using your hands in place of the paddle. There are two motions you can do with your hands to provide resistance on the surface of the water. The first is a sculling motion similar to the motion your hands make when swimming the breast stroke

Fig. 144. *A hand roll is not as difficult as it looks.* Karen Blom

(fig. 145). This provides a constant support but does not provide the same instantaneous support as slapping the water. To slap the water, it helps to lock your thumbs together so both hands act as one unit (fig. 146).

No matter which hand motion you use, allow your body to float to the surface before you start to roll up (fig. 147). This makes the water do as much of the work as possible before you begin to roll, and as long as your head and shoulders are still in

Fig. 145. *Sculling with your hands will keep them at or near the surface during a hand roll.* Karen Blom

Fig. 146. *Locking your hands together with your thumbs can make hand rolling easier.* Jon Goodman

Fig. 147. *Allow your body to float to the surface before beginning a hand roll.* Karen Blom

Fig. 148. *A hand roll in progress seen from underwater.* Karen Blom

the water, you can take advantage of their buoyancy. Once your shoulders are as close to the surface as they'll go, use whichever hand motion you have decided on, drive up powerfully with your hips, and drive down with your hands and your head (fig. 148).

It may help at first to roll quickly and continuously, carrying the momentum you gain from flipping into the hand roll. But this does not allow you to take the time to float your shoulders and head to the surface as described above and will ultimately make your roll less useful in real river situations, where it is seldom possible to carry the momentum of a flip into a continuous roll.

LEARNING THE ROLL

No one method is effective for teaching every person how to roll. Several are presented in this chapter, but feel free to develop your own to suit your particular circumstances.

Hip snap

One common learning technique is to begin by working on the hip snap without a paddle. You can use either the side of a pool or dock, another paddler's boat, or the hands of an instructor standing in the water to support yourself while learning the hip snap. The idea is to develop a roll that relies as little as possible on these props for support.

Flip over holding onto your support and bring the boat back up using your hips. Work on keeping your head down until the last minute and facing the bottom with your upper body in order to bring your stomach muscles into play. Once you are comfortable with the hip snap using a solid object for support, try using only a life jacket. If you can roll using only a life jacket, you are ready to learn the paddle motion.

With a helper standing in the water next to you, practice tucking forward on the deck and sweeping your body and paddle out to the side while still above water. The helper should hold your boat just behind you to stabilize it so you can go through the full range of motion above water.

Once you are comfortable with this motion above water, set up and flip over to your on side. Then allow the helper to position your paddle correctly and move it through the sweep and brace-up positions (fig. 149). You should still be doing the hip

Fig. 149. *A helper can position your paddle for you to help you get the feel of the paddle motion.* Bruce Lessels

motion as you practiced before. When you feel the helper moving your paddle, try to memorize the motion so you can set up yourself after a few practice rolls. Eventually, the helper can provide less and less assistance until you are rolling on your own.

Bracing lower and lower . . .

Another effective way to learn to roll is to start by learning the low brace (in a canoe) or the high brace (in a kayak). Perfect the brace with only a slight lean, then lean more and get comfortable at that angle. Continue to increase the angle until you are going all the way over and coming back up. Of course you need some sort of spotter—either another paddler or a dock or pool side—to help you up when you go too far over. The key to learning this way is to commit more and more body weight to the braces the farther over you go.

Chapter Seven

Equipment

The most common question beginning paddlers ask is, "How much does it cost to get started?" The answer is, "Between $300 and $2,000." No matter how much you spend to get into the sport, keep in mind that you will be relying on your equipment to keep you afloat, help you stay warm, and, at times, save your life. A $5 wool sweater from a tag sale works every bit as well as a new $80 pile paddling sweater, but a chintzy old bicycle helmet is no bargain when it comes to protecting your head. If you are looking for ways to save money, sacrifice fashion, style, and even comfort to some extent, but don't compromise on safety.

BOATS: DESIGN AND CONSTRUCTION

Boat design

Whitewater boat designs have become like car models. Once you decide on a particular type of boat, such as a whitewater playboat, slalom racing boat, or squirt boat, your options within that type are broad. There are very few bad boats being made nowadays. As long as you are using a boat for its intended purpose, and fit within the weight range for that design, one boat will perform almost as well as another. Blaming a mistake on the boat is generally an indication that a paddler's ego is too delicate to accept that the real culprit was his lack of technique or experience. This is not to say that there are no differences in performance between models, but just as one sports car may be faster while another takes corners better, boat designs within a given range usually trade improved performance in one area for decreased performance in another.

Whitewater boat designs can be described by referring to several common factors: volume, rocker, length, width, chine, tumblehome, flare, and freeboard.

Fig. 150. *Three kayaks showing a typical volume range from low volume (center) to medium volume (left) to high volume (right).* Bruce Lessels

A boat's volume is the amount of water that would be displaced by it if it were fully submerged. This measurement is only used to compare closed boats. Some manufacturers provide data about volume for the boats they make, but even without this data, you can roughly compare volume by eye (fig. 150).

A high-volume boat will support a heavier person and retain its stability but may be difficult for a smaller person to move around. It will ride higher through whitewater but will tend to get stuck in holes more easily, because by floating higher, it is affected more by a hole's recirculation. A lower-volume boat will often have sharp edges that can get caught by counter-currents if you are not careful. Lower-volume boats are usually more maneuverable, however, and may provide higher performance, allowing a skilled paddler to maximize his ability but at times frustrating a not-so-skilled paddler because of their low margin for error. Smaller people will find that lower-volume boats fit them better and are easier to move around.

Rocker is the amount of curvature in the hull from one end to the other when viewed from the side as in figure 151. Boats with a lot of rocker are often nicknamed "banana boats." They spin well, and it is easy to influence their end-to-end trim by leaning forward or back, but they do not go straight, or track, easily, since only a small portion of the boat is in the water at

Fig. 151. *Open canoes with varying amounts of rocker.* Bruce Lessels

any one time. Boats with little or no rocker are very fast in a straight line but tend to be difficult to turn.

The length of a boat also affects its turning ability. Longer boats tend to be more difficult to turn but track comparatively well. Shorter boats turn quickly although they are slower in a straight line. Shorter boats also tend to surf better, since they fit into the troughs of waves that are closely spaced, while longer boats tend to dive into the troughs unless you constantly cut back and forth. A longer boat often feels more stable when paddling in big water. Its tendency to bridge the waves means that each individual wave has less effect on a long boat than a short one.

Stability and speed are greatly influenced by a boat's width. The wider the boat, the more stable it will usually be. More width translates to a greater surface area in contact with the water to support your weight. A narrower boat may be faster, since it presents a minimal profile to the water as you are paddling ahead. Narrow boats often sacrifice stability for speed, however, and can be significantly more difficult to paddle.

The shape of a boat's chines determines its tracking ability and its primary and secondary stability. The chine is the area of greatest curvature in the hull when viewed in cross section (fig.

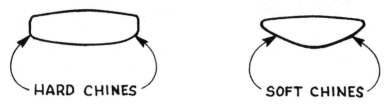

Fig. 152. *The sharpness of a boat's chines is a partial determinant of its stability and turning ability.* Noland Hisey

152). This is generally an area just below the seam line or the gunwale of an open canoe. A boat with a sharp chine usually has a flat bottom and somewhat vertical sides, making it relatively stable when sitting flat. A sharp-chined boat has a distinct point of secondary stability as well; once you have leaned past that point it is generally quick to let you know. Sharp chines toward the bow help a boat track when moving forward or into eddies, giving the eddy water a distinct vertical surface against which to push as the boat enters the eddy. More-rounded chines cause a boat to be less stable when sitting flat but more forgiving when leaned, since there is a less-defined point of no return. These boats are less affected by countercurrents but sacrifice quickness and handling.

The next three terms refer to open canoes only. Freeboard is the distance between the surface of the water and the top of the gunwales. Freeboard varies depending on the amount of weight placed in a boat. For whitewater boats, the amount of freeboard is one determinant of how dry the boat will be in waves and how much gear can be carried.

Flare in the bow of an open boat deflects water, keeping the paddler drier when paddling through waves. The boat in figure 153 has a noticeably flared bow. Tumblehome refers to the sides of a canoe turning in near the gunwales (fig. 154). Some boats have tumblehome, some don't. Those with tumblehome tend to be easier on the knuckles, since the tumblehome keeps the gunwales from interfering with your stroke.

Whitewater designs can be classified into six categories: whitewater touring boats, playboats, creek boats, slalom racing boats, wildwater racing boats, and squirt boats.

Fig. 153. *Flare in the bow of an open canoe helps keep water out.* Bruce Lessels

Touring boats are designed for general whitewater use and whitewater tripping. They usually favor tracking ability over turning ability and are stable enough to carry gear or accommodate beginner paddlers (fig. 155). Touring kayaks and closed canoes tend to be medium- to high-volume designs. Touring open canoes may have a slight V shape in their hulls that makes them track easily but decreases their responsiveness in maneuvers. A few common touring canoes are the Discovery, Explorer, and Legend. Some touring kayaks are the Quest and Taifun.

The number of playboat designs on the market has increased exponentially in recent years, as their popularity among recreational paddlers has grown. Playboats are usually of medium volume and have significant rocker (fig. 156). They

TUMBLEHOME   NO TUMBLEHOME

Fig. 154. *Tumblehome as seen in cross section.* Noland Hisey

Fig. 155. *A touring canoe.* Bruce Lessels

Fig. 156. *A whitewater play kayak.* Bruce Lessels

are not especially fast in a straight line but are extremely responsive on whitewater. They tend to be short: play kayaks and C-1s range between nine and eleven feet long, solo canoes between eleven and fourteen feet long, and tandem canoes between fourteen and sixteen feet. Because of their shortness and rocker, playboats are good at surfing waves and holes and catching eddies. They are slow on flatwater, making them suitable for extended whitewater-only trips, but frustrating on extended trips with significant stretches of flat paddling. Some popular play kayaks are the Response, Crossfire, Invader, Dancer, and Pirouette. For canoes, the Encore (solo), Prophet (solo), Dimension (tandem), Fantasy (solo), and ME (tandem), and the Gyramax C-1 are a few of the available models.

As running steep creeks has become popular, several kayaks and C-1s have been designed specifically with this area of the sport in mind. The boat in figure 157 is a creek boat in action. They spin quickly and resist diving at the bottom of steep drops due to their large-volume ends and short length. They are often good beginner boats, since they are designed for stability and ease of turning. They also surf waves and do enders well. They are very slow on flatwater but are often used

Fig. 157. *A creek boat in action.* Robert Harrison

on extended whitewater trips due to their high volume, which provides more room than is found in a playboat for storing gear. The Corsica, T-Canyon, Freefall, and Blackwater C-1 are some popular creek boats.

Slalom racing boats are generally low-volume and extremely responsive but can be difficult to paddle due to their edginess (fig. 158). The International Canoe Federation determines specifications for these boats. Slalom kayaks and C-1s must be at least 4 meters long. Slalom C-2s must be at least 4.58 meters long. Minimum widths are: 60 centimeters for kayaks, 70 centimeters for C-1s, and 80 centimeters for C-2s. Slalom designs change from year to year, as everyone tries to get a leg up on the competition. Some recent designs are the Reflex and Barcelona kayaks designed by Richard Fox; the Fanatic and Stealth C-1s designed by David Hearn and Jon Lugbill; and the Rocket Grokshark designed by Jamie McEwan, Lecky Haller, and Peter Franzoso.

Fig. 158. *A slalom boat.* Karen Blom

Fig. 159. *A wildwater racing boat in the midst of it.* Bruce Lessels

Wildwater racing boats are among the most unusual look-ing whitewater boats (fig. 159). They are very long and narrow with virtually no rocker and distinctive "wings" to meet mini-mum width requirements. They are very fast in a straight line but difficult to turn. They are also extremely tippy, making them a challenge for even expert whitewater paddlers. A few wild-water designs are the Ace C-1, the Kesako and Superstar K-1s, and the Feeling C-2.

Squirt boats share with wildwater boats a unique look (fig. 160). They are extremely low-volume and designed to perform radical stunt moves involving sinking either the stern, the bow, or the entire boat underwater. They are between eight and twelve feet long and can be classified as bow squirt boats or stern squirt boats, depending on whether both ends or just the stern are low-volume enough to do squirts. Squirt boats often sit almost entirely underwater with a paddler in them. They have very flat bottoms and extremely sharp edges. Some popu-lar squirt kayaks are the Vulcan, Bigfoot, Vampire, Hissdog, and Enigma. Some squirt C-1s are the Acrobat and the Viper.

Fig. 160. *A squirt boat standing on end.* Bill Hildreth

Boat construction

Boat construction has come a long way since the days of wood, canvas, and fiberglass. Two construction methods account for 99 percent of all boats being used on whitewater today: molded plastic and composite laminate. Molded plastic construction results in durable, low-maintenance boats and is the most popular construction method used.

Molded plastic open canoes are made of a vinyl/ABS plastic/foam/ABS plastic/vinyl sandwich called Royalex. This material comes in sheets that are vacuum molded in many different designs. Royalex canoes can be wrapped around a rock with the bow touching the stern, then returned to their original shape with a swift kick. Eventually the outside vinyl layer will wear through, especially at the bow and stern. This appears as a change in the color of the worn area, since the color of the outside layer is not carried into the inner layers. To repair or prevent this, you can add skid plates, which are available from the manufacturers. These are Kevlar pads that can be epoxied onto the boat and replaced as often as necessary. If the second vinyl layer is allowed to wear through as well, the middle foam layer will be exposed and the boat may be significantly weakened.

Molded plastic kayaks, C-1s, and C-2s are made using one of two processes: rotational molding and blow molding. Most playboats, creek boats, and touring kayaks are made from molded plastic, since weight is not at a premium as it is with racing boats, and the large number of design changes common to squirt boats are not necessary with these other boat types.

Rotationally molded boats are formed by heating and spinning a metal form into which powdered plastic has been placed. By varying the heat in specific areas of the mold, these areas can be made thicker or thinner to provide selective reinforcement. Roto-molded boats may be made of cross-linked or linear-linked plastic. Cross-linked plastic holds its shape better and is more durable than linear-linked plastic. Linear-linked boats can be repaired using plastic welding techniques but tend to lose their shape somewhat in the sun. Boats made from both types of plastic require the use of supporting foam pillars front and rear to keep a boat from collapsing on the paddler's legs in the event of a pin. Roto-molded boats are extremely durable and can be used for years without repair. They can wear through at the ends under very heavy use since the bow and stern often scrape when paddling over drops.

Blow molding produces heavier, but more rigid, boats than rotational molding. Blow-molded kayaks can be used without foam pillars, making them easier to get into and out of. In blow molding, a bulb of plastic is expanded inside a mold under heat and pressure so that it takes the shape of the mold. The plastic used in blow molding is denser than that used in rotational molding, making it more resistant to abrasion. There are not as many designs made using this process since the cost to produce each mold is much higher than for each rotational mold. There are no C-1s or C-2s presently made using this process.

Composite laminate construction involves impregnating a variety of cloths with plastic resin in a mold. Space-age materials such as Kevlar, Spectra, and graphite have significantly broadened the range of possibilities over the traditional fiberglass construction used in the sixties. This method is much more inexpensive to set up than are either of the molded plastic construction methods, making it possible for clubs and even individuals to make their own boats and experiment with their own designs. Weight can be controlled very closely using this method. Although boats as light as seven pounds have been produced for world-class racing, most composite race boats are between sixteen and twenty-five pounds. Composite recreational boats and squirt boats generally weigh in at around twenty-five to thirty-five pounds.

Two primary "layup" (construction) methods are used in composite construction. Hand layup is the simplest. It involves placing successive layers of cloth into a mold. Each layer is impregnated with resin before the next layer is added. By varying the amount of cloth used in each section of the boat, areas likely to take a beating can be selectively reinforced while other areas are kept light. In another method called "vacuum bagging," the cloth is laid into the mold all at once. A sheet of plastic is placed over the cloth and sealed to the edges of the mold. The resin is then poured under the plastic, and a vacuum pump is used to pull the plastic down tightly into the mold. The resin is moved around under the plastic with squeegees until it is evenly distributed throughout the mold. The vacuum is left on until the resin hardens. Vacuum bagging is cleaner than hand layup, and produces a stronger laminate, but it is a bit more expensive and complicated to set up. If you're interested, *The Boatbuilder's Manual* by Charlie Walbridge is an excellent source of information on building composite laminate whitewater boats.

STANDARD BOAT OUTFITTING

Foam pillars

Foam pillars run lengthwise from the cockpit to the end of the boat and support the deck of a closed boat to keep it from collapsing around the paddler (figs. 161 and 162). They also help maintain the shape of the boat, adding durability and improving performance. They are usually made of minicell or Styrofoam, although some have been made of foam core composites in lightweight applications. They should be securely anchored into the boat so they cannot fall over or come out if the boat fills with water. They should extend nearly to the end of the boat for maximum effectiveness and may extend all the way to the front of the seat in a kayak, or stop somewhere before the front of the cockpit rim to allow more room to get into or out of the boat. (A pillar can entangle your legs in an emergency wet exit, so make

Fig. 161. *Typical kayak innards showing a foam pillar in the center, hip and knee pads, and flotation bags.*

sure there is enough room left in your cockpit area to allow you to exit the boat quickly if necessary.)

Keyhole cockpits

Most recent recreational kayak designs incorporate a larger cockpit opening as a safety feature to allow the paddler to exit easily in an emergency. These "keyhole" cockpits allow most paddlers to lift one knee and bring that foot up to the front of the cockpit where it can help the paddler push out of the boat in a bow-pinning situation. Not every keyhole cockpit allows every paddler to do this. A foam pillar may prevent a tall paddler from bringing his knee up, while a shorter paddler in the same boat may easily be able to lift his knee and exit the boat.

Keyhole cockpits also allow you to twist sideways and backward out of a boat, rather than having to exit in the tucked-forward position necessary with smaller openings. While the tucked-forward position protects your face, certain pinning situations force your torso onto the back deck. In a small-cockpit boat, this body position locks your legs in the boat by forcing your knees up against the deck, while with a keyhole cockpit, you can exit the boat by simply lifting one knee and twisting to the side.

Grab loops

All boats should have grab loops of some type on bow and stern (fig. 162). They serve several functions, but the most important is to provide a handle for rescuers or victims trying to hold onto a boat in a rapid. Grab loops also provide tie-downs for cartopping a boat and handles for carrying. They can be made of rope, webbing, or molded plastic. They should be large enough that a swimmer can fit a hand into them easily, but they should not be able to twist around a victim's hand by accident. To prevent this, grab loops that are anchored in two places are safer than those that extend from a single attachment point.

Painters

Painters are lengths of rope that are attached to the grab loops on one or both ends of a boat. They help in rescuing, lining around rapids, and tying the boat to a car. Open-canoe painters are generally between eight feet and the length of the boat long. They should be secured at each end as shown in figure

Fig. 162. *A grab loop on the end of an open canoe. The attached painter has been neatly stowed under a piece of shock cord installed for that purpose.* Noland Hisey

Fig. 163. *A boat-based tow system using a stern painter and a quick-release arrangement.* Bruce Lessels

162 to prevent a paddler from becoming entangled in them while keeping them quickly accessible. Kayaks and C-1s usually don't use them at all except as a tow system as shown in figure 163.

Broach loops

Many closed boaters attach loops of cable or D rings just in front of and behind the cockpit to aid in rescuing them from a vertical pin or a broach (see fig. 170, page 161). These loops are especially useful on steep creeks where pinning is common.

Tow systems

Boat-based tow systems allow you to rescue an unconscious swimmer, a boat, or a paddle without tying up your hands. They consist of a carabiner attached to a length of rope that is attached by a quick-release mechanism to your boat (fig. 163). This mechanism must be quick and foolproof, since you must be able to release whatever you are towing if it becomes dangerous to you.

Fig. 164. *Split flotation bags for a kayak or C-1.* Bruce Lessels

Flotation

Flotation is cheap insurance for your boat. Most paddlers use flotation bags to displace water in the event of a capsize. Open canoeists sometimes use foam, but its weight makes it a less-convenient option. Flotation in a closed boat should fill the part of the boat that is not taken up by the paddler. With foam walls, you will need split flotation bags as shown in figure 161. One bag goes on each side of each wall, so you need four bags for a C-1 or kayak. Some C-2s may have room for an additional two bags between the paddlers. Boats without walls will need two bags: a bow and a stern.

Open-canoe flotation should also fill the entire boat, leaving space only for the paddlers as the boat in figure 165 shows. Tandem boats need three bags if they have room for a bag between the paddlers, two if they have room only in the ends of the boat. Solo boats need only two bags. In an open canoe, lace your flotation bags in using nylon cord or webbing that is run from gunwale to gunwale to keep them from floating out of the boat if it capsizes.

Fig. 165. *Flotation in a tandem canoe fills the entire boat leaving only room for the paddlers.* Bruce Lessels

CUSTOMIZING CANOES

In order to paddle effectively and comfortably, you must wear your boat so that each movement of your lower body translates as closely as possible into movement of the boat. You should also be able to exit your outfitting quickly and easily to prevent the possibility of entrapment. A variety of outfitting methods have been developed, none of which is right for everyone in every boat. Look for the outfitting method that fits your body and paddling style best, and don't be afraid to experiment with something new.

Thwarts are seats that extend across a canoe and are hung from the gunwales or the seams of a closed canoe (fig. 166). Their rigid connection to the boat makes them excellent at transmitting body movements, but they can catch a paddler's foot, causing entrapment, if hung too low. They are usually made of wood, although they can also be made of composites. They are tilted forward to keep the front edge of the thwart from digging into a kneeling paddler's thighs. Thwarts are often padded with foam to make them more comfortable. Hip

Fig. 166. *A thwart-type seat in an open canoe. (The lighter-colored thwarts on either side of the seat help the boat remain rigid.)* Bruce Lessels

pads on either side of a thwart can keep a paddler's hips from sliding side to side unnecessarily.

Pedestals are the other popular seat type. They consist of a foam or molded plastic seat attached to the bottom of the boat (figs. 167 and 168). They are often more comfortable than thwarts, since they can be shaped to fit a paddler's anatomy more closely than can thwarts; however, some paddlers feel they do not provide the same rigid connection to the boat as a thwart.

The normal height range for both pedestal and thwart seats is between five and twelve inches when measured from the bottom of the boat. Determining the height of your seat is a matter of trial and error and depends on a number of factors including the inherent stability of your boat design and the flexibility of your knees.

Knee pads both protect and stabilize your knees (figures 167 and 168). Any type of soft closed-cell foam works well. Minicell is probably the most common type, since it is easily available in boating stores. Knee pads can be either flat or formed to your knee. Flat knee pads allow a range of people to

Fig. 167. *A well-outfitted open canoe showing pedestal, knee cups, and thigh straps. Note location of anchor points and shoulder pad for easier portaging located below the gunwale just in front of the seat.* Bruce Lessels

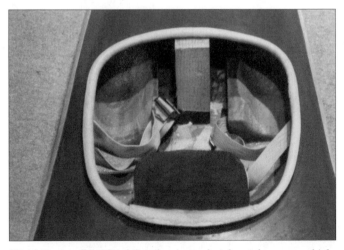

Fig. 168. *A well-outfitted C-1 showing pedestal seat, knee cups, thigh straps, and foam pillar.* Bruce Lessels

use the same outfitting, while knee cups that are cut to the shape of your knees give the best control.

Thigh straps come in a variety of types. Nylon webbing with adjustable buckles works well (figs. 167 and 168). Some paddlers use "machines," which are molded fiberglass thigh straps made to the exact shape of their legs. Machines hold you into the boat very tightly, but can be difficult to exit from and are not at all adjustable for different people who might be using the same boat. Some commercially available canoe seats have molded thigh hooks that take the place of straps.

The location of thigh straps or machines is very important. You want them to hold your knees firmly into the pads while allowing you to exit if necessary. The location of anchor points in your boat determines where the straps fall on your leg (fig. 167). Using two straps and two anchors for each strap will give you the most control by securing each leg separately. Single-strap systems with one shared anchor point in the middle do not immobilize each knee as well. Straps higher than midthigh can cause entrapment and allow your knees to move.

Some canoeists use foot pegs and foam ankle blocks to improve their fit and comfort in the boat. Foot pegs let your feet push your knees firmly into the knee pads while ankle blocks support your ankles, making kneeling for long periods more bearable. Foot pegs are usually bolted to a pedestal seat or fiberglassed into the boat, and can be made of wood, fiberglass, or aluminum.

A really custom outfitting job

Some canoe racers have experimented with an outfitting system that involves pouring expanding foam around your lower body while seated in your boat. They tape plastic around their lower bodies to keep the foam from irritating their skin. The resulting mold is a perfect fit and, once lined with a thin layer of neoprene, makes a truly custom outfitting job. There are two problems with this system. The first is that the two-part foam that is available today is not very durable and breaks down under frequent pressure, and the second is that the mold created fits your lower body so well that it can be difficult to get out of. This type of outfitting system may be the wave of the future, however, once these bugs are worked out.

CUSTOMIZING KAYAKS

Most molded plastic kayaks come almost completely outfitted. But it is important to take the time to make your boat fit you well. Some retailers offer custom outfitting, and several boat manufacturers sell customizing kits for the boats they make.

Kayak seats are generally molded of plastic or foam to fit an "average" person's contours (fig. 169). To customize a seat, you can add foam to the bottom and sides so it fits your specific contours better (figs. 161, page 152, and 170). Don't add so much padding that you significantly raise the height of your seat, since this makes the boat less stable. Some racers even glue their seats directly to the bottom of the boat rather than hanging them from the cockpit rim. Commercially available "fit kits" usually contain hip pads that can be shaved down to match the exact contours of your hips and hold you more securely in the boat. These pads can also be made easily from blocks of minicell foam.

Thigh hooks provide a point of contact between your boat and your lower thighs or the insides of your knees. Again, most boats come with some thigh hooks, although they may not fit you well. Unpadded plastic thigh hooks can be uncomfortable, so even well-fitting thigh hooks may be lightly padded to improve comfort. Be careful when adding padding to thigh hooks that you do not trap your legs in the boat. It is easy to get a leg or foot caught between a foam pillar and thigh hook on

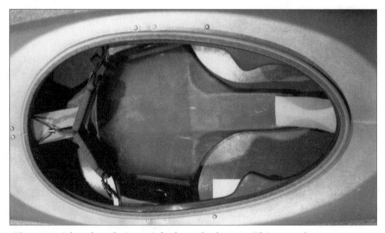

Fig. 169. *A kayak cockpit straight from the factory. This manufacturer includes a back strap as standard equipment.* Bruce Lessels

Fig. 170. *A kayak cockpit that has been padded to fit the paddler. A pack pad is being used instead of a back strap. Padding has been added to the bottom and sides of the seat and the undersides of the thigh hooks.* Bruce Lessels

the way out. One solution to this is to cut your pillar shorter so it starts farther in front of the cockpit, leaving more room between it and the seat.

Foot pedals or bulkhead footrests are essential for paddling in control. Most boats come with an adjustable footrest, although racers often install their own custom footrests by fiberglassing a bar from seam to seam in the front of the boat. Adjustable foot pedals consist of an aluminum track along which small pedals can be set at various distances from the seat. Paddlers with big feet often cut a half-moon-shaped section of the bow wall out to allow more room for their heels to meet in the center of the boat with this type of arrangement (fig. 171).

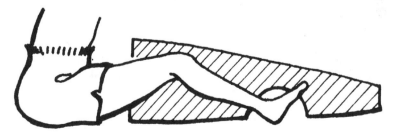

Fig. 171. *A half-moon cut out of your bow wall where your heels meet can make your feet much more comfortable if you have longfellows.* Noland Hisey

Bulkhead footbraces are popular in Europe and are catching on in the United States because of their added comfort and safety. They provide a larger surface against which to rest your feet and do not allow them to slide forward past the footrests when you hit a rock head on. The foam on the bulkhead also cushions impacts. The first boats to incorporate bulkhead footbraces were blow molded without foam pillars, but several U.S. manufacturers now produce boats with bulkheads that are cut out to fit into a foam pillar.

Back support is very important in kayak to prevent lower-back stress. Back straps or pads also help you fit more tightly in your boat by giving you something to push against when your feet are pushing off the footbraces. Without a back support, you can easily slide off the back of the seat by pushing against your footbraces. Back straps are available from several manufacturers, or you can make your own out of two inch webbing (see fig. 169, page 160). Many are adjustable, and they provide substantial support, especially for paddlers with back problems. Back pads are made from minicell or other foam that is built up behind the seat (see fig. 170, page 161). Some find this method more comfortable, but it generally does not provide as much support or adjustability as a back strap.

PADDLES

The paddle acts as steering wheel, engine, and stabilizer. Paddles are made of a wide variety of materials (fig. 172). Wood paddles are the most aesthetically pleasing and have a comfortable spring to them that eases stress on your joints and minimizes the chance for dislocations. Wood paddles require maintenance to keep them from being ruined by dry rot due to water absorption. Fiberglass paddles are stiffer than wood and often more durable, but are no match for the aesthetics of wood. Aluminum shafts are also very stiff, but they can be cold in winter and can cause joint problems because of their stiffness. Carbon fiber shafts are common on racing paddles, since they are extremely light and stiff. They are also very brittle, however, and sometimes break without warning. Their stiffness is an asset in racing, where the key is to get every ounce of power out of each stroke, but the stress they can cause on joints is a strike

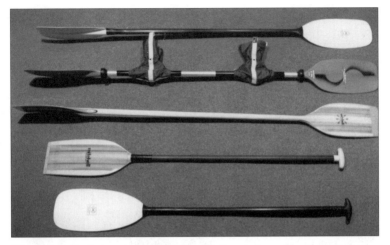

Fig. 172. *An assortment of paddles. From bottom to top: a fiberglass canoe paddle, a canoe paddle with a carbon fiber shaft and wood blade, a wooden kayak paddle, a kayak paddle with reaction injection molded blades and aluminum shaft with pogies attached, and a fiberglass kayak paddle.* Bruce Lessels

against them for everyday use. Carbon shafts are usually fitted with wood or composite blades. Blades made of an inexpensive material called reaction injection molded plastic are common on starter paddles but may tear or crack in cold weather.

Kayak paddles

Kayak paddles are double bladed, with the blades usually off-set from one another so their faces are between zero and ninety degrees apart. The offset decreases wind resistance from the nonactive blade and makes the stroke biomechanically efficient. Kayak shafts are usually oval with the long axis of the oval running perpendicular to the face of the blades. Some kayak shafts are only oval on the control-hand side. An oval shaft allows a paddler to find home position with his control hand even when he cannot see his blades.

Recently kayak paddles have been made with bent shafts known as double torques (fig. 173). These shafts put a paddler's wrists into a more natural position than do straight shafts and are supposed to decrease the chance of injury as well as use the wrist and arm muscles more efficiently. The jury is still out, but

Fig. 173. *A double-torque kayak paddle.* Bruce Lessels

most people who use double torques report improved feel and performance.

Kayak blades come in several different shapes. The standard blade shape is symmetrical. Many of the newer asymmetrical shapes are designed to get a better purchase on the water. Blade size also determines the amount of purchase you achieve on each stroke and the speed with which you can pull the paddle through the water. In general, blade size correlates to paddler size. Most of the kayak paddles in use today have spooned blades. The spoon makes them enter and grab the water more efficiently than a flat blade.

Paddle lengths of between 198 and 210 centimeters are most common for whitewater paddling. While the length of your paddle depends on many factors, including your size, arm length, how high you sit in your boat, how deep the water is in which you are paddling, and what type of boat you are paddling, here's a quick and dirty sizing method: Hold a paddle with your hands about four inches from the throat on either side; put the paddle on top of your head with your hands in this position. Your elbows should make ninety-degree angles. This method is very rough and only works well for those in the middle of the range. Experience alone can tell you exactly what length paddle you prefer. Experiment!

Canoe paddles

Canoe paddles have a single blade on one end of the shaft and a grip on the other (see fig. 172, page 163). Most whitewater paddles have t grips for maximum control, but several other grip shapes are used in other areas of canoeing and may be adapted to whitewater.

Canoe blades are usually symmetrical and flat. Many have dihedrals, or ribs, running down the center for added stiffness, although these can make them more difficult to feather. Some canoeists now use spooned blades because of the added purchase they afford. Spooned blades are a bit more difficult to feather, but they make the paddle grip the water better and are worth trying.

Like kayak blades, canoe blades come in a range of sizes to accommodate different body sizes and strengths. While it may be tempting to use a very large blade so you get the most out of each stroke, the slow stroke rate that results is not worth the trade-off. Determining canoe paddle length is best done in the boat for which the paddle will be used. Sitting in the boat on flatwater, extend your top hand to eye level or slightly higher. Now put your t grip in your top hand and your blade in the water. If the paddle is the correct length for you, the blade will be submerged up to the throat (fig. 174 shows the position of the arms with a proper-length paddle).

Fig. 174. *The proper length for a canoe paddle is best determined in your boat.*
Bruce Lessels

DRESSING FOR PADDLING

What you wear when paddling is a matter of safety, comfort, and self-image. When trade-offs are necessary among these three factors, safety should always take precedence. Proper paddling clothes ensure that you float if you swim, you stay warm in cold water and air temperatures, you are protected from bumps and scrapes, and you can paddle effectively. There is a growing market for paddling gear and, therefore, a growing number of suppliers making an ever-larger variety of products. Competition among manufacturers has improved the overall quality and design of paddling gear.

There are three essentials for paddling on whitewater: life jacket or personal flotation device (PFD), helmet, and appropriate clothing for the conditions. While some open-boat paddlers still do not use helmets, the variety of comfortable helmets available should make wearing one on anything more difficult than class II water routine, even for canoeists.

Personal flotation device

PFDs, or life jackets, serve several functions. First and most important, they support a paddler when he swims. While it may seem that a strong swimmer can get by without a PFD, swimming on whitewater is very different from swimming on flatwater or in a pool. The force of the current, the shallow rocks, and the difficulty breathing when swimming through waves leaves little time to think about staying afloat. By taking this worry off a swimming paddler's mind, a PFD provides a margin of safety that makes most swims manageable. Of course, for an unconscious swimmer a PFD could be the difference between life and death.

A second function served by a PFD is protecting a paddler's back from injury due to hitting rocks while upside down. This becomes especially important when running small shallow creeks. A snug-fitting PFD can also add significant warmth to your abdominal and chest areas, contributing to the overall warmth of other paddling clothing by insulating these vital areas.

PFDs designed specifically for use in whitewater rescues incorporate additional features such as a quick-release harness system to tie a paddler into a rope during a strong-swimmer rescue. They also may have a quick-release tow system to pull a boat or unconscious swimmer, and some are fitted with quick-draw throw bags attached backpack-style. All these accessories are easy to disengage from if a swimmer or boat is threatening to put the rescuer in danger. Rescue life jackets are specialized pieces of equipment that can be dangerous if misused but have the potential to save a life when used by a skilled paddler.

PFDs come in a variety of designs (fig. 175). Most are approved by the U.S. Coast Guard and can, therefore, be used to fulfill Coast Guard requirements that a boat have one PFD aboard for every person. This is sometimes an issue for whitewater boaters on rivers such as the Youghiogheny in Pennsylvania, where the river runs through a state park and rangers at the put-in check for appropriate equipment. Some racing designs and imported PFDs are not Coast Guard approved but are frequently used on whitewater, and many meet International Canoe Federation standards, or the standards of the country in which they were produced. Whether they are safe enough or not is a question each paddler needs to answer for himself. The Coast Guard rates jackets as types I

Fig. 175. *Three popular PFD designs. From left, a low-profile squirt vest, a rescue vest with quick-release tow system, and a standard whitewater vest.* Bruce Lessels

through V, depending on their buoyancy, style, and purpose. Most whitewater jackets are types III or V.

PFDs run the gamut from low-float racing designs to high-flotation cruising and rafting designs. Kayakers should look for a PFD without a lower flotation panel, since this interferes with a sprayskirt and gets in the way of paddling. Canoeists can use the longer PFDs but often use the shorter designs as well, since they tend to be more comfortable and provide greater mobility. PFDs with flotation over the shoulder make portaging more comfortable by providing a shoulder pad, and give additional protection to your shoulders, but tend to be restrictive around the arms. Some PFDs with large armholes feel like you aren't wearing a PFD at all. Regardless of the style you choose, be sure it fits properly and is adjusted correctly every time you wear it. If your ill-fitting PFD rides high when you swim, you'll find yourself drinking more of the river than you want.

Helmet

Needless to say, protecting your head is a top priority. Of the many whitewater helmet designs on the market, most are at least adequate for general paddling (fig. 176). Whitewater helmets are made of a variety of plastics and composite laminates. They are usually lined with foam or have a plastic suspension system to cushion a blow. A helmet should protect your entire skull, from the forehead to the temples, and back to the rear of the skull. It needs to fit snugly and should not ride back where it can expose your forehead or off to the side exposing a temple. Many biking helmets, while fashionable, do not provide the full-head coverage needed for whitewater.

Fig. 176. *Whitewater helmets provide varying degrees of protection and comfort.* Bruce Lessels

Keeping warm

Your body loses heat many times faster in water than in air. A swim that would be routine in the summer can be very serious in the early spring when both the water and air temperatures are much lower. A few general principles of dressing for paddling are:

- **Don't wear cotton.** Cotton fibers absorb water and keep it next to your skin, making you colder rather than warmer. Polypropylene, wool, Lycra, neoprene, and nylon pile make effective nonabsorbent insulating layers.

- **Dress in layers.** Start with a wicking layer next to your skin to draw perspiration away from your body. Your second layer should be an insulating layer. A pile sweater, or an old wool sweater, works well here. Pile union suits are available for wear under a drysuit and are excellent as a first or second layer. The top layer should provide wind and water protection. A waterproof paddling jacket and/or pants or a drysuit works well as a top layer.

- **Keep your head warm.** You lose 70 percent of your heat through your head. Simply wearing a hat can contribute significantly to your ability to stay warm. Pile or neoprene helmet liners are excellent head warmers. Helmets also provide significant warmth—those without drain holes, and with a continuous foam lining, are the warmest. For the budget-conscious paddler, a swimmer's bathing cap will do a tremendous amount to help keep your head warm.

- **Wear wind protection.** Wind draws heat away from your body at an amazing rate. A simple paddle jacket or other type of nylon shell can often mean the difference between a comfortable paddle and a miserable survival experience.

Wetsuit

By trapping a layer of warm water between itself and your skin, a wetsuit keeps you warm even in very cold water. Wetsuits are made of neoprene with a nylon lining on one or both sides (fig. 177). Most wetsuits made today have nylon on two sides for strength.

Fig. 177. *A farmer john wetsuit and a paddle jacket will keep you warm in most conditions.* Bruce Lessels

Wetsuits can constrict your movement and make it painful to kneel in a canoe for extended periods because of the bulk of neoprene behind your knees. To solve this problem, some canoeists cut out the backs of the knees on their wetsuits.

Most paddlers today use farmer john–style wetsuits made of 1/8-inch neoprene. These look like overalls, with either long or short legs and no arms. Over this, you can wear a sweater and paddle jacket or drytop to supplement the insulation on your torso.

Drysuit

Unlike a wetsuit, a drysuit keeps water out. Aside from your own perspiration, you should have virtually no water inside a well-fitting drysuit after paddling. Drysuits are made of coated nylon with latex seals at the neck, wrists, and ankles and usually have a waterproof entry zipper on the front or the back of the chest or a seal between the top and bottom (fig. 178). While more expensive than a wetsuit, a drysuit is the ultimate in cold-weather wear, since it creates a total barrier between you and the water. It allows you to wear insulating layers that stay dry and therefore fully effective. Drysuits must be custom fitted to each individual by stretching or cutting the latex seals at the wrists, ankles, and neck. These seals are somewhat delicate and can tear if treated roughly, or exposed to sunscreen, bug repellent, cosmetics, or too much ultraviolet light. Maintain them regularly by treating them with a silicone vinyl treatment such as Armor-All or Seal Saver. They can be replaced when they wear out.

Fig. 178. *A one-piece front-entry drysuit. The latex seals at the wrists, ankles, and neck are covered by protective cuffs.* Bruce Lessels

Drysuits come in one- and two-piece models. The one-piece models have zipper entries, while the two-piece models have roll seals to join the top and bottom. Two-piece drysuits are more difficult to put on but are somewhat more versatile, since the top can be used alone. Drytops provide a near-perfect seal against water hitting a decked boater, whose sprayskirt protects his lower body, which is inside the boat. They are excellent for boaters with strong Eskimo rolls in areas with cold water and warm air temperatures where a full drysuit is too much.

Paddle jacket and pants

For paddling in moderate air and water temperatures, nylon paddle jackets and/or pants worn over an insulating layer are an excellent option. Made of waterproof nylon with either neoprene or elastic seals (see fig. 177, page 170), paddle jackets and pants keep the spray off and provide wind protection but will not keep you as warm as a drysuit or a wetsuit in the event of a swim.

Hand protection

There is a variety of options available to protect your hands from cold. Neoprene gloves or mittens are probably the warmest, but they don't allow you to feel the paddle. Latex gloves that attach to a drysuit can be lined with thin polypropylene gloves, but they tear easily and don't let you feel the paddle.

Pogies attach to the paddle shaft (see fig.172, page 163), leaving your bare hand to grip the paddle while the insulation and wind protection provided by the pogie surrounds your hands. Pogies are made of nylon or neoprene. Some of the nylon models are lined with pile to make them warmer.

Footwear

While bare feet are fine inside the boat, some form of footwear is important to prevent injuries when walking on shore or swimming a rapid (fig. 179). Neoprene booties provide a combination of insulation and foot protection. River sandals are becoming the footwear of choice for raft guides and paddlers in warm climates, although they offer limited foot protection.

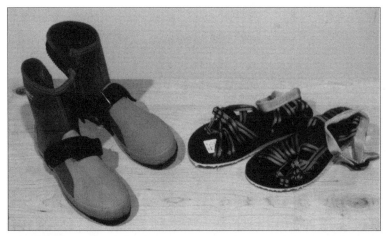

Fig. 179. *Two types of river footwear: neoprene booties and river sandals.*
Bruce Lessels

They are not a good choice for c-boaters, however, since the straps cut into a canoeist's feet in the kneeling position. They should fit well and attach securely to your feet. Thongs that are only attached at the toe are not appropriate river footwear. An old pair of sneakers and wool socks are fine for moderate temperatures. Be sure your footwear does not prevent you from exiting your boat and that your feet cannot become trapped under a canoe thwart or inside a kayak.

Sprayskirt

A sprayskirt provides a watertight seal between the paddler and the cockpit rim. Most skirts are neoprene with elastic cord or a rubber rand to hold them onto the boat (fig. 180). Skirts made of nylon are cheaper and more durable but not as dry.

The ideal skirt is almost taut in front of the boater when it is on the rim, so that water does not puddle and push the skirt down. A skirt that fits well at the waist should be snug but comfortable when you are fully dressed for paddling. You should be able to thump your fist on the center of the skirt in front of you without its popping off the rim if the skirt fits properly. Every skirt should have a grab loop in front that allows an upside-down boater to release it quickly and easily. Many boaters tie a whiffle golf ball to their skirt grab loops to

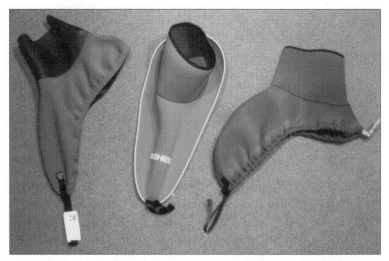

Fig. 180. *Three popular sprayskirt attachment methods. From left: rubber rand, sewn shock cord, and adjustable shock cord.* Bruce Lessels

make them easier to find by feel in the event of a wet exit. Extremely tight skirts and those with a sticky rubber rand are for experts only, since they can be very difficult to get off in an emergency.

CARTOPPING YOUR BOAT

Car rack systems have become extremely sophisticated and are made to fit every type of car imaginable. But to tie a boat to a car doesn't take a $500 rack. Any sturdy rack that has at least two crosspieces running above the roof will do. Some systems have uprights to allow several boats to be stacked next to each other (fig. 181). These are very handy for carrying multiple boats. Cradles are also available to protect your boat from damage while being transported.

Tie a boat down in at least three places: one rope on each of the two racks and one rope from the bow of the boat to the front bumper of the car. This protects not only your boat but also other drivers who might not be expecting a flying kayak on the interstate.

Fig. 181. *A simple car rack with uprights to accommodate more boats stacked on their sides.* Bruce Lessels

CARRYING AND EMPTYING YOUR BOAT

Whitewater boats generally weigh between twenty-five and seventy pounds dry. There are several carrying methods that distribute their weight well and prevent injury to your back. As in picking up any heavy weight, be careful to keep your back straight and lift with your legs as much as possible.

The most common carrying method for closed boats and solo open boats is to put the cockpit over your shoulder (fig. 182). You can also simply pick up the cockpit and walk with the boat hanging from your straight arm (fig. 183). Tandem boats generally have a portage thwart located at the boat's center of balance that fits over your shoulders, making it possible for a single person to carry one (fig. 184). Two people can carry a tandem boat by each taking an end and either lifting the boat to their shoulders or walking with the boat hanging from straight arms as described above for kayaks.

One person can pick up a tandem canoe with a center carrying thwart, using the correct technique. Start with the boat right side up on the ground in front of you. Standing next to the

Fig. 182. *A common method of carrying a closed boat.* Karen Blom

Fig. 183. *Another common carrying method. This method is uncomfortable on long carries.* Bruce Lessels

Fig. 184. *Carrying a tandem canoe alone using a portage thwart.* Karen Blom

center of the boat, grasp one side of the center thwart with each hand. Now sit back slightly, lifting the boat up onto your thighs (fig. 185). Use the weight of the boat to counterbalance your body's weight as you sit back. From this position, thrust your hips forward and up while bringing the boat quickly onto your shoulders with your arms (fig. 186). Most of the lifting force should come from the hip thrust.

Fig. 185. *Getting ready to lift the canoe onto the paddler's shoulders.* Peter Franzoso

Fig. 186. *Thrust your hips forward while quickly lifting the boat onto your shoulders.* Peter Franzoso

Fig. 187. *Emptying a closed boat by balancing its weight on the paddler's leg.*
Karen Blom

Emptying your boat can be a real back breaker as well if you're not careful. A boat that is full of water is far too heavy to lift, so start by rolling it on its side or slowly lifting one end to start the water running out of it. Once most of the water is out, you can turn it all the way upside down and drain the remaining water by either tilting it toward one end, then the other, as shown in figure 187 for a closed boat, or simply letting the water run out for an open boat.

Chapter Eight

Managing Risk

Everyone makes mistakes on whitewater: Experts pin, beginners swim, and intermediates push their limits. The key is to be alert and prepared to handle a problem if one arises. Most paddlers like the intense focus that dangerous conditions require. If there were such a thing as risk-free whitewater, the sport would die out in a matter of years. By evaluating and managing the inherent risks, a thoughtful paddler can decide just how far to push himself and just how much backup he'll need if something goes wrong.

The safest boater is not the one with the most equipment but rather the one with the best judgment and the most paddling skill. A prevented accident has never gotten out of control. Ropes, carabiners, and pulleys are only last resorts and may not save a paddler who has made a mistake. Likewise, a paddler with excellent skills and minimal rescue equipment may be better off than a less-experienced boater carrying winches, pulleys, and ropes but who cannot roll.

Whitewater rescue is mostly common sense; the most practical solution is often the simplest. Yet rescuers often forget this in the rush to set up complex rope systems to perform rescues that could have been done more quickly simply by lifting one end of the boat or using a paddle to extend a rescuer's reach. While the rope tricks may be fun and carrying the equipment gives some boaters a feeling of security, too many paddlers get too involved in the mechanics of a rescue, ignoring the victim or missing a much simpler, quicker solution. The time to experiment with new rope tricks or set up complicated Z-drags is during a rescue clinic; in a real-life river rescue, there is only time to think of practical, quick solutions. For more information read *River Rescue* by Les Bechdel and Slim Ray (AMC Books, 1989).

SWIMMING IN WHITEWATER

Swimming in easy to moderate whitewater is no big deal if you're prepared, but it can be scary and dangerous if you don't follow a few simple rules. It helps to practice swimming on flatwater and in easy whitewater to learn to react correctly in a relatively safe environment (fig. 188). When you practice swimming, make sure other boaters are around to help if you get into trouble.

The first thing to think about if you find yourself swimming is to get on your back with your feet up. Your feet are high enough when you can see your toes on the surface in front of you; this minimizes entrapment risk. Foot entrapment is one of the most common causes of death among river runners. Small cracks between rocks, trees, or other material lying on the bottom of the river can catch the foot of a paddler who is trying to stand. Once your foot is trapped, you are powerless to help yourself and are usually forced by the current into a position that does not allow you to breathe.

The standard defensive swimming position on whitewater is to lie on your back with your feet on the surface pointed downstream (fig. 189). This position allows your feet to fend off rocks and puts you in a position from which you can see what's coming up downstream of you. From this position you can

Fig. 188. *Practicing self-rescue.* Noland Hisey

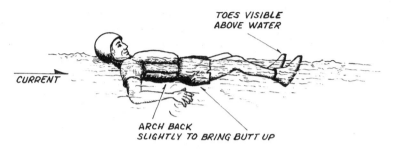

Fig. 189. *The standard defensive swimming position.* Noland Hisey

back-stroke with your arms to ferry your body to one side of the river or the other.

After exiting from your boat, attempt to hold onto it and your paddle. Move to the upstream end of your boat, and hold boat and paddle in the same hand, using the other hand to swim or hold onto a rescuer's boat. Remember, your safety comes first. If you are not comfortable with the situation, or are injured, abandon your equipment and get yourself to shore as soon as possible.

When you first come out of your boat, assuming this defensive position may help you collect yourself and assess the situation, but take an active role in your own rescue as soon as possible. Once you have come up with a course of action (a shore or boat to swim toward), aggressively pursue it by swimming strongly toward your goal. In deep enough water you may find it easier to swim by turning over onto your stomach. In shallow water, you can stay on your back, and backstroke or sidestroke to ferry yourself to one side or the other. Self-rescue will not only help you get to safety as quickly as possible but will also help your rescuers by taking some of the burden off them. A strong swimmer can use eddies and other currents to help him get out of the river or over to one shore.

When swimming over large vertical drops or pourovers, it sometimes helps to curl into a ball as you crest the drop, since going feet first can push your feet deep and cause entrapment. As soon as you are clear of the drop, resume your normal swimming position. The disadvantage to curling up is that you expose your backside.

BOAT-BASED SWIMMER RESCUE

A paddler in his boat can often assist a swimmer by offering the victim his stern grab loop. The swimmer holds onto the grab loop in one hand and his gear in the other while kicking with his legs to help the rescuer get to shore (fig. 190). The rescuer's boat can help the swimmer both psychologically, by letting him know someone is there to help, and physically, by offering additional buoyancy to help the victim stay above water in waves and by providing additional power to help the victim get to shore. If the water is especially big or the victim is injured, the rescuer may tell the swimmer to crawl up on the stern deck of the boat to get farther out of the water.

As a victim, you must respect the rescuer's safety and abide by his wishes. Never grab a rescuer or his boat near the cockpit area, since this may make him flip, adding to the problem. Always let go of the boat if the rescuer tells you to, and don't forget to thank him.

Tow systems attached to the boat or PFD can be used to rescue boats or injured swimmers. The paddler clips the carabiner from the tow system into the victim or boat and allows the tether rope to feed out to its full length. The paddler then tows the

Fig. 190. *Helping a swimmer to shore.*

victim or boat to safety. If the victim or boat threatens to endanger the rescuer, he can quickly release the tether, setting the boat or victim free. You should practice with any tow system before using it in a rescue situation.

WADING RESCUES

When done properly, wading can be a safe, quick method to get to a paddler who is pinned or otherwise stranded midriver. Using the techniques described below, you can wade in water up to chest deep. The primary advantage of wading is that it involves virtually no setup, making it useful in getting to victims who are in immediate danger. Always set up a safety back-up if you are going to attempt a wading rescue. This can be a throw rope on shore downstream of the rescue or a boater who can keep an eye on the rescuers. Wading requires practice and should be used at the discretion of an experienced paddler, since bottom configuration, rapids below the rescue site, and several other factors could make a wading rescue very risky.

In one-person wading, face upstream and walk slowly across the river. Use your feet to feel the bottom and plan each step, resisting the urge to lunge, since this can result in a foot entrapment. You can significantly improve your ability to wade by using a paddle as a support (fig. 191). Slice the paddle blade

Fig. 191. *One-person wading using a paddle for support. Note the eddy formed downstream of the paddler.* Karen Blom

into the water parallel to the current and rotate it ninety degrees as it moves down, allowing the current to pin it to the bottom. Move a step or two, then move the paddle.

Adding a second person for support greatly increases your stability and the depth of water you can wade. One person stands upstream facing downstream, and the other stands downstream facing upstream. The two rescuers grasp the shoulders of each others' PFDs. One person should move at a time, telling the other when he is stable so the other person can move. The upstream rescuer creates an eddy in which the downstream rescuer can wade, making it much easier for the downstream rescuer to maintain his footing. The downstream rescuer in turn supports the upstream rescuer from his stable position.

Three- or four-person wading creates a tremendous eddy and is the most effective technique in deep or powerful current. The rescuers face each other, forming a ring, and each one grasps the shoulders of the PFDs of the people on each side of him. The ring moves as a unit around the upstream-most person, who stays stationary until the next person is stable in the upstream position. The eddy created by this technique can be used to lessen the current's force on an entrapment victim, and the downstream rescuer in the ring can reach behind him to get ahold of the victim if necessary. A single rescuer can also wade out in the eddy of the ring, using either a paddle or the back of the downstream rescuer's PFD for support. This rescuer can attend to the victim once the wading ring is above him.

IDENTIFYING AND DEALING WITH HAZARDS

The first principle of safety is to keep out of trouble. And, since trouble comes, as a rule, in standard packages, it is worthwhile to look at some of them.

Dams

Man-made dams are often very dangerous due to the regularity of the holes they form (fig. 192). The height of a dam is not necessarily an indicator of its danger. Low-head dams with drops of only two to three feet can be as hazardous as fifteen- or twenty-foot dams; the holes they form can be as regular and violent

Fig. 192. *A low-head dam with a regular hole below.* Bruce Lessels

as those formed by higher drops. The danger of weirs or dams is not in the initial drop from the upper to the lower level but in the hydraulic that follows. Watch a log caught in a hole; it will roll over and over at the base of the drop, at times being sucked under only to shoot back up where the current emerges and be carried back to begin the cycle again.

Another danger inherent in man-made structures of any type on a river is the possibility of debris lodged in the riverbed. Broken dams often have exposed reinforcing rod, timbers, and spikes. Although some broken dams are frequently run without injury, the possibility of such debris must be taken into account.

Running dams requires tremendous experience and judgment. Always scout at the level at which you are going to run a dam, and it is often useful to check it without water to look for debris that may exist below the dam. Unless you have the experience necessary to evaluate such runs, or the dam is frequently run and has been proven relatively safe, the best policy is to carry. Do not attempt to run a dam where there is even a small chance of being trapped. Self-rescue may be impossible, and rescue by others may be difficult or too late.

If you have no alternative to running a potentially dangerous dam, be sure to run it straight, since turning sideways will immediately trap you in the hydraulic; paddle to keep up speed as you drop over, then drive forward when you reach the water below. This is where you can be deceived into believing you have made it over safely. Not yet, for you must still power out of the hole. If you get caught in the hole and leave your boat, your best chance of swimming is sometimes to dive with the main current at the base of the dam, letting it help you get under the recirculation of the hydraulic. Remember that the surface water feeds back toward the dam, while the deeper water continues downstream. If you have difficulty swimming out of a hole, try changing your position from a spread eagle to a tuck and back again. The idea is to introduce some randomness into an otherwise regular hole.

Strainers

A strainer is any obstacle that allows water to pass through but can trap a boat, swimmer, or debris floating down the river. Typical strainers are trees that have fallen into the river (fig. 193), trash racks at the intakes of hydroelectric plants, logjams, and rocks with holes going through them.

Probably the most common form of strainer is a downed tree on the outside of a river bend. Erosion on the outside of the bend causes trees on the bank to fall into the river. The current

Fig. 193. *Trees often form dangerous strainers. The best approach is to stay away.* Bruce Lessels

also pushes a boater to the outside of the turn, so there is an increased chance of boater meeting strainer. Strainers are one of the most insidious hazards on whitewater. They may be invisible under the surface of the river or sticking up in full view.

Being alert for and avoiding them is by far the best option. But if you do find yourself floating toward a strainer in your boat with no possibility of avoiding it, try getting your bow up and paddling over it if it is on or just above the surface. If it is well above the surface and you are coming at it broadside, lean toward it and try to climb out of your boat onto it. By all means, avoid the temptation to lean upstream away from a strainer, since this will cause you to flip immediately with severe consequences. If you are swimming toward a strainer with no possibility of avoiding it, turn onto your stomach with your head pointed downstream and swim aggressively at it. When you reach the strainer, quickly climb up onto it.

Undercut rocks

Rocks that have been eroded away or are undercut on the upstream side present a hazard, because there is generally little if any pillow to keep you away when you are in your boat (fig. 194). Out of your boat they can be deadly, since they trap debris

Fig. 194. *An undercut rock.* Bruce Lessels

and other objects that float down the river such as unwary swimmers.

The geology of a riverbed will often alert you to the possibility of undercut rocks. When the riverbed is made of limestone, sandstone, or other easily erodible rocks, chances are good there will be some undercuts. Even if the geology does not indicate a chance for undercuts, keep an eye out for them, and try to find out from local paddlers or guidebooks if any exist before running a new stretch of river.

Avoid undercuts. The presence of an undercut rock in a rapid you are scouting may be reason enough not to run the rapid.

SAFETY AND RESCUE GEAR

A few pieces of simple equipment are all that are necessary for most river situations (fig. 195). A first-aid kit, whistle, throw rope, a couple of prussiks, and a couple of carabiners are sufficient for all but the most involved rescue and can easily be carried by a kayaker or canoeist. Other useful rescue equipment

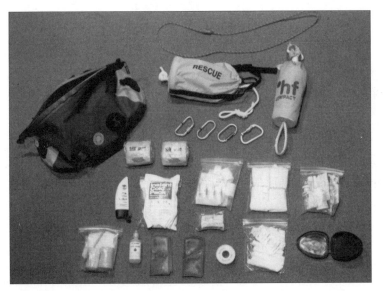

Fig. 195. *Basic safety gear: a first-aid kit (laid out next to its waterproof bag), locking and nonlocking carabiners, two models of throw bags, and a prussik loop.* Bruce Lessels

includes pulleys, winches, additional ropes, saws, knives, and rescue life jackets.

First-aid kit

A first-aid kit should contain as many multipurpose items as possible, since space and weight are of the essence. Familiarize yourself with the kit you are carrying, and be sure all supplies are kept in a truly waterproof container such as a waterproof bag, ammo can, or other waterproof box. A typical whitewater first aid kit for day trips might contain the following:

bandages	gauze pads
tweezers	first-aid tape
scissors	antibiotic cream
Ace bandage	splints
sugar source	heat packs
paper and pencil	cold packs
sanitary napkins	emergency phone numbers
rubber gloves	quarter (to make an emergency phone call)
CPR mask	triangular bandages
duct tape	matches

Whistle

Voices carry poorly over the sound of whitewater, so whistles help communicate in emergencies. Most paddlers attach a whistle to their PFD in the vicinity of the shoulder so it is easy to blow when needed. Be careful not to overuse a whistle. It should be blown only in an emergency, so boaters do not get too accustomed to hearing it and ignore it during a rescue. The standard signal for help is three long blasts.

Throw rope

Throw ropes extend your reach during a rescue. They consist of a rope stuffed inside a nylon bag. Stuffing the rope inside the bag keeps it out of your way and ready to throw at a moment's notice. There are several excellent throw bags on the market. Your choice should be based on a number of factors. The length of the rope varies from fifty to seventy-five feet and determines the size of the throw bag. A closed boater may prefer a smaller bag with a shorter line since it fits more easily in a boat. Two types of rope are commonly used in throw bags: polypropylene and a space-age fiber called Spectra. Polypropylene ropes float and are generally easy to tie knots in but are not very strong and stretch a tremendous amount under loads. This makes them useful for rescuing swimmers but less effective for pulling boats off rocks or performing rescues that involve tensioning the rope. Spectra also floats and is many times stronger than polypropylene for the equivalent diameter. It stretches very little under load and does not absorb water. It is excellent for rescuing swimmers or boats and can withstand tremendous loads before breaking. Its drawback is its cost, which can be more than double that of polypropylene.

All paddlers should practice throwing a rope. You can throw either underhand, overhand, or sidearm and should hold the free end of the rope in your nonthrowing hand. Always keep several feet of rope with you so you can pay some out when tension is put on it. Before you throw, make sure you have a secure footing where you are standing or a place to sit down if you are being pulled off your feet. Never wrap a rope around your wrist, foot, or any other part of your body, since the chance of becoming entangled is great. Never tie a rope to a rescuer unless he is wearing a quick-release harness.

Think carefully about where you set up a throw rope (fig. 196), since a poorly placed rope can do a swimmer more harm than good. Imagine where the victim will end up after he takes hold of the rope. Try to set it up to swing the victim into an eddy; do not set a rope so that the victim pendulums into a hole, strainer, undercut, or other hazard.

Prussik loops

Prussik loops are short lengths of rope that have many uses. Tied in a prussik knot on another rope (figs. 197, 198, and 199), a prussik loop can act as a brake in a Z-drag (see fig. 207, page 198. To make a prussik loop, make an eight- to ten-foot length of rope into a loop using a double fisherman's knot (see page 196) The resulting loop can be worn like a belt around your waist and attached with a carabiner.

Fig. 196. *Set up a throw rope below a drop where you can pendulum a swimmer into an eddy. Be careful that the rope can't pendulum him into a hazard.* Bruce Lessels

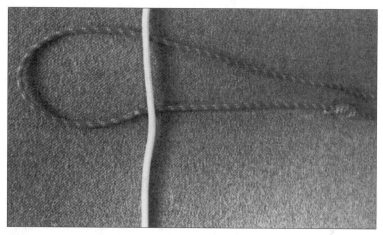

Figs. 197, 198 and 199. *A prussik knot, showing how it's made.* Bruce Lessels

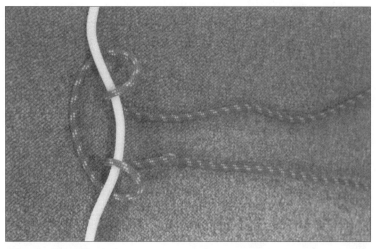

Fig. 198. Bruce Lessels

Fig. 199. Bruce Lessels

Carabiners

Carabiners are snap links originally designed for mountain climbers that are also useful to paddlers. They can be used to secure gear inside a boat, to clip into the grab loop of another boat during a rescue, or to attach a haul rope to a pinned boat. They come in locking and nonlocking models and in a variety of shapes. Most paddlers carry at least two. A couple of manufacturers make extra-large carabiners that can be clipped onto a paddle shaft or cockpit rim to provide an attachment point. According to the manufacturers, these carabiners are not strong enough to use in haul systems.

A few useful knots

Every paddler should know how to tie a few simple knots: the bowline, figure eight, and double fisherman's.

The bowline (figs. 200 and 201) is used to create a loop. It does not jam easily but can slip when tied in a new rope. To avoid this, tie off the free end with an overhand knot.

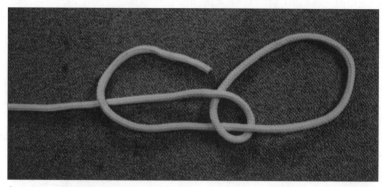

Figs. 200 and 201. *Tying a bowline. Note the completed knot is tied off with an overhand around the rope to prevent the bowline from slipping.* Bruce Lessels

Fig. 201. Bruce Lessels

Figs. 202 and 203. *Two types of figure eight knots being tied. The knot on the right is used when the pull is in the middle of a rope. The knot on the left is used when the knot is on the end of the rope, and one or both ends are being pulled in the same direction. Use a figure eight instead of a simple overhand loop, because it can be undone after being tensioned.* Bruce Lessels

Fig. 203. Bruce Lessels

The figure eight family of knots is especially handy because of the variety of applications to which they can be adapted and the ease with which they can be tied. They also release easily after being loaded, making them useful when hauling boats off rocks. Figures 202 and 203 show the two most common types of figure eight knots.

Figs. 204 and 205. *Tying a double fisherman's knot.* Bruce Lessels

Fig. 205. Bruce Lessels

The double fisherman's knot is the best way to join two ends of rope together if you're not concerned about taking them apart again. Figures 204 and 205 show how to make a double fisherman's knot.

UNPINNING BOATS

A canoe or kayak solidly wrapped around a rock is testimony to a river's tremendous force. Even slow-moving water can pin a boat so it can only be removed with great effort. Unpinning can turn into a real ordeal, taking many hours and using up large amounts of equipment. Always keep in mind that the boat is irrelevant compared to the safety of the people. If to unpin a boat you put yourself or others at too great a risk, reconsider your plan. If the weather is cold, or the hour late, it may be better to leave the boat and have the unfortunate paddler walk out.

Always be aware of your condition and the condition of other members of your group as the rescue proceeds, watching for signs that indicate people are getting too cold, or hypothermic, such as uncontrollable shivering, slurred speech, and irritability.

As you formulate your plan, start with the simplest solution and work toward the most complex. Often pushing or pulling on the boat in the proper direction will get it off. If this does not work, try the ten Boy Scout, or "armstrong," method next: Attach a rope to one end of the boat so the direction of pull coincides with the way the current wants to take the boat, and get as many people pulling as possible. To add force, add people. The next option is to use a vector pull. Tighten the rope around a tree or rock using a trucker's hitch (fig. 206), and pull at an angle to the rope. You can attach a second rope to the first to pull with more people. If this too fails, try a Z-drag. This is a method of gaining mechanical advantage by setting up a pulley system on the rope itself. A simple Z-drag is shown in figure 207. By adding Z-drag on top of Z-drag, you can increase the mechanical advantage.

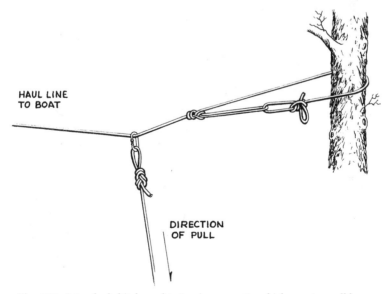

HAUL LINE
TO BOAT

DIRECTION
OF PULL

Fig. 206. *A trucker's hitch used to tension a rope to which a vector pull has been applied.* Noland Hisey

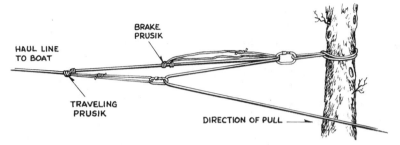

Fig. 207. *A single Z-drag.* Noland Hisey

When pulling on any sort of haul system, protect the rescuers in the event the rope breaks and the energy stored in it sends it flying back at them. There are several ways to do this. The first is to redirect the pull on the rope, so you are hauling at right angles to the line. This can be done by running the rope you are pulling on through a carabiner attached to the anchor point to change the angle of pull. Another way to protect the rescuers is to hang a life jacket or bag of rocks on the tensioned rope between the boat and the first rescuer. The inertia of this object will absorb the force of the rope and stop it where it hits the object, keeping it from injuring the haulers.

UNIVERSAL RIVER SIGNALS

Because of the noise made by rapids, verbal communication often breaks down. The American Whitewater Affiliation has developed a system of river signals that are nearly universally understood.

STOP (fig. 208): Potential hazard ahead. Wait for "all-clear" signal before proceeding, or scout ahead. Form a horizontal bar with your paddle or outstretched arms. Move up and down to attract attention, using a pumping motion with paddle or flying motion with arms. Those seeing this signal should pass it back to others in the party.

HELP/EMERGENCY (fig. 209): Assist the signaler as quickly as possible. Give three long blasts on a whistle while waving a helmet or life vest over your head in a circular motion. If a whistle is not available, use the visual signal alone.

Fig. 208. *The signal for STOP.* American Whitewater Affiliation

Fig. 209. *The signal for HELP.* American Whitewater Affiliation

Fig. 210. *The signal for ALL-CLEAR.* American Whitewater Affiliation

ALL-CLEAR (fig. 210): Come ahead. (In the absence of other directions, proceed down the center.) Form a vertical bar with your paddle or one arm held high above your head. Paddle blade should be turned flat for maximum visibility. To signal direction or a preferred course through a rapid around obstructions, lower the previously vertical "all-clear" by forty-five degrees toward the side of the river with the preferred route. Never point toward the obstacle you wish to avoid.

GROUP ORGANIZATION

In a disorganized river group, each paddler might as well be paddling alone. A significant margin of safety comes from group organization and communication. The suggested minimum number of paddlers on a river is three. Although some experts paddle in groups of one or two on water that is within their limits, this is not recommended for beginning paddlers.

A standard river-running order is to assign a lead boat and a sweep boat. The lead boat goes first down each rapid. He should be the boater who knows the river best or the most experienced boater. No other boater should pass the lead boat. The sweep takes up the rear and should be the next most experienced boater. He never passes another boater and should have the first-aid kit if the group has only one, since he will always be upstream of the accident site and can get to it quickly if necessary. Every boater keeps the boater behind him in sight. If you lose sight of the boat behind you, or see him stop, stop immediately, and do not proceed until you see the boat behind you again. Using this approach, a group can be sure each member can communicate with every other member at all times.

Section II

Advanced Techniques

Once you have a handle on the basics, there are few limits in whitewater except those you impose on yourself. Some paddlers find challenge in running the most difficult water, while others strive for the ideal ender on class III and IV rapids. Still other paddlers enjoy maneuvering down a fast-moving class II–III river. Advanced paddling is constantly being redefined as paddlers on the cutting edge come up with new equipment and techniques to meet ever more difficult challenges. This section covers a wide range of advanced techniques, but these are not by any means the only ones out there. Hopefully the intermediate to advanced boater will be inspired to try some of these variations of the sport of whitewater, and this section will get him or her started.

Chapter Nine

Playboating: Whitewater Tricks

Playboating is a broad category of techniques that, as in freestyle skiing or circus acrobatics, use a few basic physical principles to push the limits of the sport. Playing a rapid may mean performing cartwheels in your boat or balancing on edge in a hole with no paddle. The variety of techniques is as broad as your imagination. Playing a river means taking advantage of every little current, tuning in to the shape of each wave and hole, and using the river's flow to make your boat defy the laws of gravity. The best playboaters make it look more than easy; they make it look like the river is doing it for them. And that's closer to the truth than some may believe. Playboating is a measure of your understanding of the river and of your trust in yourself. Sticking your nose into a hole that will blast you out of the water requires that you know your limits, the limits of your equipment, and the nature of the river. All philosophy aside, playboating is addictively fun.

ENDERS, PIROUETTES, AND POP-UPS

When your boat does a cartwheel in a rapid, it's called an ender. In a pop-up, your boat stands on end but doesn't go all the way over to complete the cartwheel. Enders and pop-ups are for the acrobats among paddlers (fig. 211). By sticking the nose of your boat into a hole, eddy wall, or wave trough, you can be launched vertically out of the river, sometimes completely clearing the water with your bow, and land either upside down in an ender or right side up in a pop-up or pirouette.

The shape of the river feature is key to determining whether an ender or pop-up is even possible. For a hole or eddy

Fig. 211. *An ender for the crowds.* Bruce Lessels

wall to give you an ender, the water coming into it must fall more or less vertically where you will put your nose. The water at the base of the hole or eddy wall must be deep enough that your bow will clear the bottom of the river. Plastic boats make the best depth probes, since even if the water below is not deep enough, you're unlikely to break your bow finding out.

To do an ender or pop-up is simple: Paddle your boat into the hole from downstream, and let the water coming vertically over the ledge force your bow down causing your stern to rise out of the water. If you're at the correct angle to the current, your boat will stand on end vertically as your stern comes up. The more parallel your boat is to the current coming into the hole, the more vertical your ender will be. If the downward force from the water coming over the ledge is powerful enough, you may go all the way over end-for-end and land upside down in an ender. If the current is less powerful, your stern may only go up and come back down again in a pop-up.

To ender on a steep wave, maneuver your boat parallel to the current while surfing. Once your bow is pointing into the trough, simply let your boat slide into the trough, and enjoy the launch you get (fig. 212).

Fig. 212. *Getting a pop-up from a wave.* Bruce Lessels

Waves are constantly changing shape. Some that are marginally steep enough will only ender you if you time the fluctuations right. On such a wave, you often need to surf back and forth making frequent, sharp cuts until you feel it steepen. Then bring your boat parallel to the current, and dive into the trough. It helps if you start diving into the trough from high up on the wave, since this gives you time to accelerate before hitting the trough and makes a more dynamic ender. If a feature is barely powerful enough to give an ender, you can help it along by leaning forward as you put your bow into it.

Pirouettes are enders where you land right-side up. When the boat is at the top of its trajectory, you can spin it around its long axis by doing a sort of vertical sweep or crossbow draw as illustrated in figure 213. Although your boat lands where it would in an ender, by spinning it about its long axis in midair, you can cause it to land upright rather than upside down.

Do a rear ender by putting your stern into a hole or the trough of a wave. Because you can't see what's happening as well as in a front ender, you feel like you're being shot out of a cannon. Other common ender variations are:

Fig. 213. *To pirouette, take a crossbow draw at the height of an ender so your boat will land right-side up.* Bruce Lessels

- **Cartwheels,** where you do successive front and rear enders. These are often not planned and may result from trying to punch too powerful a hole. You can sometimes do planned cartwheels on the edge of a large hole by alternately sticking your bow and stern into the hole and pirouetting or rolling quickly after each ender.

- **Waving enders,** where you take one hand off the paddle and ham it up for the crowds.

- **No-paddle enders,** where you throw your paddle away in midair, and pray your hand roll works.

HOLE SURFING TRICKS

Hand surfing

The ultimate test of balance is to hand surf a hole (fig. 214). Once you are comfortable in the hole, try taking your paddle off the water, and see if you can maintain your lean without it. When you've mastered this, place the paddle on your bow deck (fig. 215), and eventually throw it to a friend in an eddy or on shore. To throw your paddle away completely, you should have

Fig. 214. *Hand surfing a hole.* Karen Blom

Fig. 215. *Getting used to balancing without the paddle.* Karen Blom

a reliable hand roll or be willing to swim below the hole if you flip. Also remember that a hole that is easy to surf without a paddle may not be as easy to exit without one.

When you have mastered the balance and confidence necessary to hand surf, let your imagination run wild. Try juggling, reading a book, drinking a soda, or even doing headstands in an open boat. Whitewater rodeos are showcases for such tricks, and as their popularity has grown, the variety of tricks paddlers think up has expanded as well.

Spinning in holes

Spinning 360 degrees in a hole helps you learn to shift your leans quickly and fine-tunes your feel for surfing. To spin in a hole, start to paddle out one end, then as the boat starts to come parallel to the current, spin quickly using a forward or reverse sweep, and shift your lean to the new downstream edge just as you go past parallel. The goal is to remain in the hole after the spin. The trick is to clear the hole quickly with your upstream end. An unsuccessful spin can easily turn into a pop-up or ender that pushes you out of the hole if your upstream end gets caught in the current entering the hole. On the other side of the coin, if you let your boat climb too far out of the hole, the recycle may not be strong enough to pull you back in after you've spun.

HAND PADDLING

The latest technique for the paddler who has tried it all is hand paddling. Using webbed gloves, or swimmers' hand paddles, skilled kayakers and C-1ers can do practically any move without a paddle that can be done with one (figure 216).

Fig. 216. *Hand paddling is for the paddler who's tried it all.* Bill Hildreth

Fig. 217. *Boogie boarding: a minimalist technique.* Slim Ray

BOOGIE BOARDING

Small surfboard-style "boogie boards" are also catching on with advanced paddlers who have outgrown their boats (fig. 217). This minimalist approach to running whitewater is really a controlled swimming technique. Boogie boarders wear knee and elbow pads, full wetsuits, helmets, and, of course, PFDs. Many of the same maneuvers that can be done with a boat can also be done with a boogie board. Visibility is significantly reduced over that of a kayaker, so boogie boarders need to scout from shore more often than boaters.

Chapter Ten

Squirt Boating

This area of the sport grew out of slalom racing in the early 1980s. As slalom racers began using lower- and lower-volume boat designs, they learned to slice their sterns underwater to speed up turns. They did this by breaking the rule that says you should always lean to the inside of a turn. Recreational boaters caught on to the possibilities for river running, and a major new whitewater technique was born. A whole boating subculture has developed around squirting with its own lingo, equipment, and personalities.

Squirting requires a low-volume boat with a very flat or concave deck and sharp edges, such as the boat in the middle in figure 150 (see page 141). Boat design and volume are so critical that squirt boats are sold in several "cuts" with different volumes to accommodate different size boaters. If you decide to get into squirting, remember these boats are significantly more difficult to paddle than ordinary surface boats. Most squirt boats are so low-volume that boaters get into them on shore and do a "seal entry," sliding into the water after attaching their sprayskirt on land since they would sink if they tried to attach their sprayskirt in the water. The added difficulty of paddling these boats, along with the tight fit they require, makes them more dangerous than surface boats. A number of fatal pinnings have occurred in squirt boats over the last several years, so don't get in over your head; if you are able to paddle class IV in a surface boat, start squirt boating on class III or easier water first.

SQUIRTS

The foundation of all squirt moves is the basic squirt. This can be done from the stern or the bow. To do a stern squirt in flatwater, paddle forward to gain momentum, then reach way

Fig. 218. *A stern squirt in a kayak.* Bruce Lessels

behind you and begin a reverse sweep while leaning back. At the same time, lean the boat away from the sweep so the outside edge digs into the water. The spinning motion of the boat along with the angle of attack of your outside stern edge to the water will cause your stern to dive and your bow to rise out of the water (fig. 218). The amount you lean is critical. Too much lean will stall the squirt, and you may take a dunking, while too little lean will not allow your outside edge to dive, resulting in a flat spin. To keep a stern squirt going after the reverse sweep has reached the bow, feather the stroke into a duffek. The duffek can then be feathered back to the stern again, where you are then ready to start another reverse sweep. Throughout this maneuver, maintain a constant lean.

Stern squirts can also be done using a forward sweep. The principles are the same, except that with a forward sweep you lean toward the paddle. The tendency on this type of squirt is to rely on your paddle for support, turning the forward sweep into more of a sweeping high brace, which reduces your control over the boat's turning.

Bow squirts work according to the same principles as stern squirts. In a kayak, from a stationary position in flatwater, reverse sweep on one side while leaning toward that side and forward. When you have used up the reverse sweep, go quickly to a forward sweep on the other side. This forward sweep should be similar to the vertical forward sweep/crossbow draw described above under pirouettes (see page 206). Once the boat is sitting vertically on its bow, maintain its position by subtlely varying your forward and back leans, and using your paddle to do a sort of vertical low brace (fig. 219). To do this vertical low brace, you need a paddle that is feathered forty-five degrees or less, since at times you will be bracing on both blades at once.

To do a bow squirt in a C-1 requires very precise balance and a reliable roll. On flatwater, paddle forward to build up some speed, then allow your boat to start turning gradually toward your on side. Once your boat has begun turning toward your on side, quickly reach across the bow to do a cross draw while leaning forward and slightly toward your off side. The action of dragging your bow back to the off side after allowing it to pick up momentum to the on side helps the bow dive. Bow squirts in a C-1 are all-or-nothing moves. Your bow either dives right down and leaves you standing on end, or you find yourself counting trout before you know what happened. This type of bow squirt can also be done in a kayak using the sequence of strokes and leans described above. It is a good balance exercise for kayakers who are used to having a brace on both sides.

Fig. 219. *A bow squirt in a kayak using a vertical low brace to maintain the position of the boat.* Bill Hildreth

You can use the force of the river to your advantage in a squirt boat by driving your upstream edge into the oncoming current to do a bow or stern squirt. This significantly increases the dynamic feeling you get from the move. To turn a simple peelout into a stern squirt, approach the current as you normally would in a peelout, but just as you cross the eddy line, initiate a powerful reverse sweep on the downstream side while leaning upstream. This is a very committing move, since the upstream lean relies on the force of the reverse sweep to keep it from becoming an upstream flip. The upstream lean also must be very precise—too much lean can result in an even faster flip than on flatwater. Be prepared to get wet when learning this move. Once you've felt the force of the river launch you out of the water in a stern squirt, however, you'll never go back!

Bow squirts are also more dynamic on whitewater than on flatwater. Ferry out of an eddy until you are at least a few feet from the eddy line. Then quickly pull the bow back toward the eddy using either a crossbow draw or a reverse sweep on the side of your boat that is closest to the eddy as shown in figures 220 and 221. Lean forward and toward the eddy (upstream). Pulling your bow back toward the eddy and upstream will cause either a very dynamic squirt (fig. 222) or an equally dynamic flip. Learning to bow squirt on whitewater is a great way to cool off on a hot summer day.

Fig. 220. *Initiating a bow squirt by pulling the bow back toward the eddy with a cross draw.* Karen Blom

Fig. 221. *Bringing the paddle over the deck.* Karen Blom

Fig. 222. *And, the result.* Karen Blom

Combining bow and stern squirts into the same move is called cartwheeling. Start with a stern squirt, then smash the bow under by letting the stern squirt fall to one side and doing a powerful reverse sweep (kayak) or cross draw on that side. At the same time, change your lean from backward to forward. Once you are in a bow squirt, do a cross draw to a forward sweep to bring yourself back to a stern squirt.

BLASTS

Once you have basic squirt technique down, one of the most dynamic moves you can do is called a blast. Blasting takes advantage of the current differential in a hole, pourover, seam, or eddy wall to hold your boat in a sustained squirt position as shown in figure 223. Blasting allows you to surf a hole as you would a wave, with your boat parallel to the current.

The best place to learn to blast is in a hole with a well-defined recycle formed by a low-angle ledge. While you can blast vertical holes and pourovers, they are not ideal for learning due to the consequences of missing a blast and the difficulty of side-surfing them. When you have found a low-angle hole to learn in, get into a side-surfing position in it, and practice taking your paddle off the water for increasing periods of time until you feel comfortable surfing without your paddle supporting you. Now to get into the blast, either do a reverse sweep with your upstream blade (for offside C-1s and kayaks) or a forward sweep with your downstream blade while leaning back and continuing to lean downstream. Your stern will slice under the hole, and your bow should rise above the water entering the hole. Once in this position, maintain it using stern rudders and forward sweeps. In some holes, you may find there's a sweet spot where your boat blasts especially well, while others are

Fig. 223. *Blasting a hole.* Joan Hildreth

more uniform and allow you to cut from one end to the other by varying your angle slightly and ferrying in a blasting position. The steeper the hole and the more powerful the recycle, the more vertically your boat will sit when you blast.

With a bow squirt boat, you can also perform bow blasts. From a side-surfing position, turn your bow downstream using either a reverse sweep on the downstream side for kayakers and on-side C-1ers, or a cross draw for off-side C-1ers. At the same time, lean forward and continue to lean downstream. Maintain this position using either reverse sweeps/vertical low braces or forward sweeps. Once you have mastered both bow and stern blasts, you can combine them by going from one to the other. This move is similar to performing cartwheels (which are described above on flatwater) in a hole.

Blasts also work well when surfing ocean waves. Once the wave you are surfing breaks, you can blast the hole formed as the wave rolls in to shore.

SPLATS

To splat, you paddle above a rock with a well-developed pillow and squirt just as your bow is about to hit the rock (fig. 224). When it works, your boat stands on end just in front of the rock,

Fig. 224. *Splatting a rock.* Shirley Griffith

and if the pillow is strong enough, boat and rock never touch. When it doesn't work, a splat can easily turn into a pin. Splatting is one of the most dangerous squirt techniques if not done in the right place. For this reason, you should choose your rock very carefully. Undercuts are definitely out. Even what look like nice round rocks are sometimes undercut below the surface of the water, so check carefully before trying a splat. Rocks with upstream faces that angle downstream are good for splatting, because they tend to surf you off to one side if you flip. Rocks with debris on them, or narrow channels to one side or the other, are usually not good for splatting. Rocks that stick out from shore and only have current on one side are less likely to cause a pin, since the current is all moving the same way and will tend to take your boat that way as well if you flip.

ADVANCED SQUIRTING AND WHERE TO FIND MORE INFORMATION

The techniques described here are just a small fraction of those that are used by expert squirt paddlers. Screwups, meltdowns, and mystery moves are a few of the ever-increasing number of advanced squirt techniques. Many of these techniques (and the sport of squirting itself) were pioneered by the Snyder brothers on the Upper Youghiogheny in western Maryland. Jim Snyder has written an excellent book that goes into detail on all aspects of squirting and is humorously illustrated by cartoonist William Nealy. *The Squirt Book: The Manual of Squirt Kayaking Technique* is published by Menasha Ridge Press.

Chapter Eleven

Steep Creeks

When the rains come or the snow melts, some paddlers go "creekin'," heading for the steepest, most jumbled stream in the area where what had been merely a trickle the day before is now raging whitewater (fig. 225). Steep creeks typically have gradients of over 100 feet per mile, with some exceeding 300 feet per mile. They tend to be narrow and fast. Typical flows range from 200 to 1,500 cubic feet per second (cfs), although

Fig. 225. *Steep creekin'.* Karen Blom

some creeks are considerably larger. Their rapids often contain one big drop after another and are sometimes interspersed with waterfalls or large slides. A few creek runs even have runnable rapids underground or in caves. Boat design is important for running creeks. The design characteristics described in chapter 7 under creek boats are crucial in preventing bow pins, especially on some of the more extreme creeks. The techniques discussed in this chapter are explained in the context of steep creeking, but many also apply to everyday river running.

At the upper end of steep creeking is some of the most challenging and dangerous water run. When running water of this difficulty with so many rocks and shallow drops, the risk of serious injury due to direct collisions with rocks is high. European paddlers often wear elbow and shoulder pads and face shields similar to those worn by football players. In steep creeking, as in whitewater paddling in general, the amount of risk you take is a personal decision. On any steep creek, the potential for downed trees that cross the entire river is great, since creek beds tend to be narrow with steep banks. Group size becomes critical on creeks with few eddies, and at times groups of three or four paddlers may be the maximum that can safely paddle together.

RUNNING LEDGES AT AN ANGLE

To run a drop with a shallow landing, angle your boat slightly one way or the other (fig. 226). This will keep your bow from diving as much at the base of the drop by effectively shortening your boat. At times you may have no choice but to land on a rock. In this situation try to have your bow hit the rock as much on the bottom of the hull as possible. The key is not to hit the rock head on with the point of your bow, a move known as "pitoning." This can result in a smashed bow, broken ankles for kayakers, or bruised thighs for C-boaters. Pitoning can also result in a bow pin, where the nose of your boat is trapped between rocks at the base of the drop. This is a very dangerous situation. By hitting the rock with the bottom of your boat, you can often skip off the rock, making the landing relatively soft and carrying some momentum into the next move if necessary.

Fig. 226. *Angling your boat makes it effectively shorter as it goes over a drop, minimizing the danger of bow pinning.* Karen Blom

A second situation in which paddling with an angle over a drop is useful is when running a drop with a steep, grabby hole at the bottom where it is not possible to pancake (see below). By running the drop at an angle, you present a shorter boat to the hole and keep it from grabbing your stern, which can result in a violent rear ender. In this case, you would also want to run the drop with considerable speed to ensure that you clear the recycle of the hole with the speed you carry over the drop.

PANCAKING (OR BOOFING)

Pancaking refers to the feeling you have when you land with a flat boat at the base of a drop: You feel like a flapjack that has just been flipped in the pan. Often a pancake is accompanied by a loud boom as your boat's hull smashes down on the water all at once; hence its other name: boof. You can pancake off almost any size drop, as long as it is steep enough or has a fast enough entry. Spouts (drops where the water gradually steepens as it falls) are difficult to pancake, since it's nearly impossible to build up enough speed to clear the falling water. Vertical drops, where the water falls abruptly, are ideal for pancaking. The advantage of pancaking off a drop is that it requires very little water at the base of the drop, allowing you to land in six inches of water without touching bottom. It is also useful on falls with bad holes at the bottom. By pancaking you clear the hole and avoid a thrashing. Keeping your bow dry also gives you more control after a drop—especially important if there is another drop immediately downstream.

On an ideal drop, you can pancake simply by paddling straight over with enough speed and leaning back (fig. 227). However, most drops are far from ideal. On drops that are less than vertical, angling your boat often helps it clear the falling water, since this makes your boat effectively shorter. A sweep on the way over the drop often helps get your bow up, and leaning back and lifting the bow with your legs just as you crest the lip of the drop is always important.

Fig. 227. *Pancaking off a drop.* Shirley Griffith

Where you run a drop has a lot to do with how easy or difficult it is to pancake. Often the water is steepest near the rocks that border the chute on either side. By paddling at about forty-five degrees off the drop right next to the rock, you can sometimes land in the eddy clear of a bad hole that would otherwise ender you if you tried going straight through it. Some drops have launching pads where the water is steeper than in other places or the ledge extends farther out over the drop.

On waterfalls, it is sometimes possible to pancake too much. Landing perfectly flat off a twenty- or thirty-foot falls can compress your spine or cause the seams to split on a fiberglass boat. To keep yourself from doing this, don't lean as far back, or lean your boat slightly to one side as you hit the bottom, causing it to slice into the water a little.

ROCK JUMPING

Some rapids offer no alternative to jumping straight over a rock to avoid a hazard (fig. 228). While this sounds like a crude method of running a rapid, it can be done with style if you think about it, and it's a lot of fun if you choose your rock carefully. Obviously, rock jumping is best done with a plastic boat or a very heavy-duty fiberglass boat. You can jump rocks that stick

Fig. 228. *Rock jumping can be done with finesse.* Karen Blom

out of the water by as much as a foot or so if they are shaped right and have a good approach. Ideally, find a saddle or depression in the rock where it is lowest to the water. A clear approach helps too, since it gives you time to gather speed to carry into the jump.

The technique is simple; paddle straight at the rock where you want to jump it, and lean back to keep your bow up as you take your last stroke before hitting the rock. Sometimes you only need to jump the edge of a rock, or you can jump it where there's a little water coming over it. Both situations allow you to maintain more speed through the move.

RUNNING FALLS

Jumping over waterfalls is certainly one of the most visually spectacular whitewater moves, and often one of the most adrenalin pumping as well (fig. 229). Waterfalls up to sixty feet have been run in canoes and kayaks, but above about twenty feet, the impact you and your boat take is tremendous, and you need to seriously question your sanity. Not every waterfall is runnable. In fact, most are not runnable, and those that have been run successfully have often been scouted for months before being

Fig. 229. *Jumping a waterfall.* David Hearn

attempted. To make a first descent of a waterfall, you should be an expert paddler with years of experience, since an error in judgment can be fatal. No matter what the situation, always scout a waterfall from shore before running it, since you cannot see the base from your boat.

Several factors contribute to the runnability of a waterfall. The landing must be clear and deep enough. If you think your boat may end up diving at the bottom of the falls, make sure there is enough depth to allow your entire boat to submerge vertically. If the landing requires you to pancake to avoid hitting bottom, make absolutely sure the launch and the shape of the falls will allow you to pancake. A shallow landing makes a falls very dangerous no matter how good the launching area is, since any mistake can cause you to piton extremely hard at the bottom. Ask yourself if the hole at the base of the falls will be a problem. Can you clear the recycle? Some drops have a recycle going both upstream on the downstream side of the falls and downstream on the upstream side of the falls behind the curtain of water. This type of double hole can trap a swimmer. Finally, look at the approach and the runout. Will you be able to get up enough speed as you near the edge, or will you have to maneuver around too many eddies and rocks? Is there a clear area at the foot of the drop to rescue? If the falls leads right into another rapid, will you have time to recover if something goes wrong with your run? These are some of the many factors that figure into an expert's assessment of whether or not to run a falls. If you are not an expert, only try falls that you have been successfully run in the past at appropriate water levels.

Once you have determined a falls is runnable, choose your route carefully. Whether you take the path that will allow you to pancake most easily, or that which sends you through the weakest part of the hole, pick out a few clear reference points to let you know where you are on the approach. A line that appears obvious from shore can completely disappear from the boat, where often all you see is a horizon line and the tops of trees. On the way over, be careful not to hold your paddle in front of your face—more than one boater has eaten his paddle at the base of a drop. It is better to hold your paddle either to the side or just over your head, although the latter position puts your shoulders at some risk of dislocation.

Fig. 230. *Duckies are ideal for running steep drops and slides.* Joan Hildreth

DUCKIES AND THRILL SEEKERS

Although this book is not about inflatables, inflatable kayaks are increasingly being used to run shallow, rocky creeks and deserve mention here as an alternative to traditional boats. Normal Duckies are constructed of two outside tubes that are attached at each end (fig. 230). The floor is inflated and is self-bailing, allowing water to run out through grommets or lacings at the base of the tubes. Thrill Seekers are Duckies with a piece of foam between the floor and the paddler and thigh straps to help the paddler control the boat. Thrill Seekers provide additional protection from rocks, and their extra rigidity makes them more maneuverable. Inflatable technique is similar to the kayak techniques described above. They are more difficult to roll than a kayak, but it is possible to jump right back into an inflatable if you wet exit, even in the middle of a difficult rapid.

Chapter Twelve

Attaining
(Paddling up Rapids)

Most people think of whitewater paddling as getting down rapids in control. Yet paddling up rapids, or attaining, can be equally exciting and challenging. Attaining requires more precision than paddling downstream, since being a few inches off line can mean the difference between climbing a drop and getting rejected. Attaining is not as strength-dependent as it might seem. In fact, precise technique often wins out over strength. Climbing a rapid makes you aware of every feature, no matter how subtle, since it is often the minor advantage you gain from using a small eddy or wave that makes it possible to attain a drop. Attaining also helps you develop a can-do attitude. Seeing someone paddle up a steep vertical drop tends to open your mind to new possibilities.

To climb a rapid, look for the weak spots. The easiest kind of rapid to climb is one with a succession of eddies where you can ferry from the top of one eddy to the tail of the next one up (fig. 231). Once in the next eddy, simply paddle up it to the top and ferry to the tail of the next eddy. Try to paddle in upstream-moving water or at least dead water, avoiding downstream-moving current. Often the tail of a small hole or pourover, or even a line of boils coming off the bottom of the river, is enough to allow you to paddle upstream.

Carrying the momentum you gain from an eddy into the current is crucial. Vary the rhythm of your strokes by paddling easily up the eddies, then taking a few quick, hard strokes just as you are about to enter the current again. If you must stop near the top of the eddy, don't try to regain speed from that position. Instead, drop back so you have room to take at least a few strokes before entering the current. For canoeists especially,

227

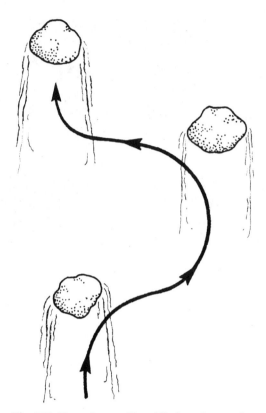

Fig. 231. *To attain a rapid, paddle from the top of one eddy to the tail of the next.* Noland Hisey

a well-timed push off the rock with your paddle at the top of the eddy can add valuable momentum to a move. With practice and an aluminum, wood, or fiberglass tip on your paddle, you can pole off rocks that are almost perfectly smooth, exploiting small nubbins to gain a hold with your blade.

You can save yourself considerable work by reading the water carefully when attaining. Read each wave or hole to see where it leads. A wave that angles up a drop can often be the key to climbing an otherwise unattainable rapid (fig. 232). By blasting out of your eddy onto the wave, and taking quick strokes on its crest, you can sometimes climb a large drop with only a few strokes and relatively little effort.

Fig. 232. *Following a wave up a drop.* Karen Blom

J leans come in handy when climbing very steep drops. Lean your boat on edge and your body back when you take the last stroke before engaging the drop. This way you present less surface area to the falling water, causing your bow to rise up over the drop due to its buoyancy, rather than to dive from the downward force of the drop. The more extreme the lean, the more effective it will be in keeping your bow up, but the more difficult it will be to keep your balance.

Once you have crested the lip of a steep drop, leaning slightly forward again helps bring your boat back into a level position from which it maintains speed better than with the stern low in the water. On a truly vertical drop, the attainment either goes smoothly and quickly or you are immediately rejected once you engage the drop.

A smooth, quick attainment, then, involves paddling in the eddy to gain momentum, leaning back and on edge just as you take the last stroke in the eddy, then reaching over the drop to take the next stroke in the water above it, and shifting your weight forward as you crest the lip. If all has gone well, your stroke above the drop should pull you solidly up to the next level, and you should be able to take a few more quick strokes to paddle away into the upper eddy.

You may find yourself in limbo for a moment at the crest of the drop. If you have gotten this far, you can often pull it off by continuing to paddle with quick, powerful strokes. To hesitate at this point is to guarantee defeat. It may not feel like you are going anywhere, but a little perseverance can often get you over the drop.

Drops that fluctuate are especially interesting to attain. At times they may be three feet high, while a few seconds later they may be only a foot high. This phenomenon is common on high-volume rivers or rivers at high water. To attain a drop where the water level is fluctuating, watch the water carefully for a few minutes before acting. Try to get into its rhythm so you can make your move when the drop is at its most attainable, then move quickly when you see it fluctuating to your advantage.

Chapter Thirteen

Racing

Whitewater racing is a tremendous way to improve your general boating skills without taking on difficult or dangerous water. It requires the same precision and mental control needed on class V whitewater, yet it takes place on class II–IV rapids. You can get into racing on any level from local beginner races to international and Olympic competition. You can race once a year or every weekend, in anything from a high-tech slalom or wildwater boat to a recreational canoe or kayak. The American Canoe Association's National Slalom and Wildwater Committee governs the sport of whitewater racing in the United States. They publish calendars of the races being held in each region and nationwide and provide insurance for race organizers. The national headquarters of the American Canoe Association is located at 7432 Alban Station Boulevard, Suite B-226, Springfield, VA 22150.

The four primary types of whitewater racing in the U.S. are open-boat slalom and wildwater and closed boat slalom and wildwater. Open-boat racing uses open canoes that are often designed specifically for each discipline or class. Open-canoe racing is done from the local to the national level. Closed-boat racers paddle C-1s, C-2s, and kayaks. Closed-boat races cover a spectrum of skill levels from beginner competitions, known as C/D races, through national and international events. Slalom races are tests of speed and precision. The competitors paddle through twenty-five gates hung from wires over a rapid. Their scores are based on their overall times plus a number of penalty points that are assessed for hitting or missing gates. Wildwater races are point-to-point contests where competitors are scored solely on their elapsed times down the river.

Former U.S. Whitewater Team coach William T. Endicott has written several excellent books on both slalom and wildwater closed boat racing: *To Win the Worlds* and *The Ultimate Run* on slalom, and *The Danger Zone* about wildwater. These books are available from the author at 6237 Broad Street, Bethesda, MD 20816. Another source of information about closed-boat racing is *Whitewater Racing* by former U.S. team members Eric Evans and John Burton. It is out of print, but if you can find an old copy in your club's library, or somewhere else, it is a useful reference. A good book about open-canoe racing is *Canoe Racing* by Heed and Mansfield, which is available through Acorn Publishg, Syracuse, NY.

SLALOM RACING

Racing down a slalom course is like riding on a knife's edge. The constant trade-off between speed and precision requires intense concentration and physical effort. Yet the experience of reaching the finish line on your first penalty-free run or paddling in a national or world championship is well worth the effort.

Slalom courses were originally designed to simulate difficult rapids. Gates are defined by wooden poles hung from wires above the water (fig. 233). The paddler must pass between the poles in a specified direction. By setting gates in places paddlers might not otherwise think of going, course designers can challenge expert paddlers on class II or III water. Of the twenty-five

Fig. 233. *Slalom gates are hung above the river on wires suspended between the banks.* Bruce Lessels

gates on a slalom course, some are negotiated by paddling downstream through them and some by paddling upstream. The upstream gates are generally set in slower-moving water or in eddies, while downstreams can be placed almost anywhere. Downstream gates are indicated by green poles while upstreams are red. Each gate is numbered and must be run in numerical order. The number plaque that hangs from the cross-bar connecting the two poles has the number of the gate on both sides. On the side from which a boater exits the gate the number is crossed out with a red line, while on the entry side of the gate the number stands alone. Gates are a minimum of 1.2 meters wide and may be as wide as 3.5 meters. The line connecting the two poles is referred to as the gate line.

The bottom of each pole is hung slightly above the surface of the water. This allows low-volume racing boats to "sneak" under the poles with one or both ends, shortening the path a racer takes in and between gates and minimizing penalties taken by hitting a pole with the boat. The ability to sneak gates was one of the primary motivations behind designing ever-smaller slalom boats in the late 1970s and early 1980s. Pivot turns or squirts also resulted from this trend toward lower volume, although the ability to do pivot turns did not initially drive low-volume boat design.

Penalties are assessed for hitting a pole or missing or incorrectly negotiating a gate. A five-second penalty is added to a racer's score if she hits a pole with any part of her boat, body, or paddle. A fifty-second penalty is incurred for missing a gate completely, running a gate out of sequence, or improperly negotiating a gate. Improper negotiation includes entering a gate from the wrong side, running a gate upside down, reaching only part of your head in the gate, or getting only your head in the gate without the boat. At high-level races, the winners are usually clean; that is, the best runs are penalty-free.

Running times on slalom courses vary from two minutes or less to five or six minutes on especially long open-boat courses. International closed-boat courses are becoming shorter each year to accommodate television crews who want to film each racer's entire run with as few cameras as possible. Yet even at two minutes, slalom racing combines aerobic and anaerobic effort, making it a sport that requires both endurance and strength.

The better of two official runs of the slalom course is a racer's counting run. At major races, only one practice run on the racecourse with the gates in their proper places is allowed, although racers often arrive at a site days or weeks early to get to know the water and to practice moves that might be set in the real racecourse. At most local races, the course is open for several hours or days before the race, and practice is allowed on the gates as set for the race. This is a great opportunity to build your skills on real whitewater gates.

Downstreams and offsets

Downstream gates in current can be very easy or exceedingly difficult depending on their exact placement and the placement of the gates above and below them. For a downstream gate in the middle of an otherwise clear channel, you simply paddle through, timing your strokes so that you miss hitting the poles as you take the stroke that pulls you through the gate (fig. 234). This generally means making sure you reach your paddle through the gate just before your body passes between the poles.

To run a series of downstream gates that are offset from one another across the river is more involved. Anticipate the next

Fig. 234. *On a simple downstream gate, timing your strokes so you don't hit the gate is the major concern.* Bruce Lessels

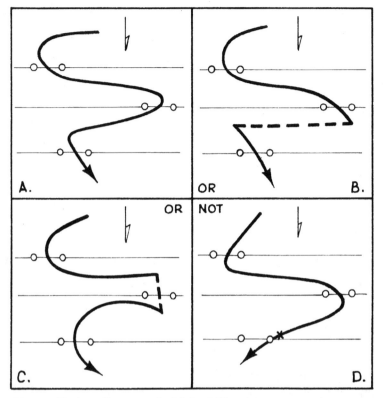

Fig. 235. *Various offset strategies.* Noland Hisey

gate by turning above the gate you are about to negotiate, so when you pass through that gate you are already heading for the next one (fig. 235). There are two reasons for this. First, turning in a gate is risky—you can easily hit a pole. Secondly, by turning before the gate, you can gain momentum toward the next gate as you are passing through the first one. This is especially important in fast current, since the current is like a conveyor belt. Not only must you paddle across the current from one gate to the other, but you must do it before the conveyor belt has swept you downstream of the next gate. On extremely fast water with gates that are offset far across the river from one another, it is sometimes necessary to turn upstream between gates and ferry to keep yourself from being swept too far downstream.

When offset gates are right on top of one another but set relatively far across the river, racers sometimes find it easier and faster to simply back ferry from one gate to another (fig. 235 B). This move requires that you stop your momentum and set an angle with your boat quickly just as you pass through the first gate, then backpaddle a few strokes to get to the next gate, and switch back to forward paddling to continue down the course. Generally, if a back ferry requires more than a few strokes between the gates, it is faster to do the move directly; that is, by paddling forward between the gates, even if it requires you to turn your bow upstream and ferry.

Another way to run tight offsets is by spinning reverse in one of the gates (fig. 235 C). By spinning you momentarily check your momentum, giving yourself time to turn toward the next gate. You also turn over fewer degrees if the next gate is far to the side. Once you have spun reverse, you are in a good position to ferry to the next gate if necessary, although often by slowing your momentum spinning allows you to avoid ferrying and lets you immediately peel out into the next gate.

A simple-looking downstream can be very difficult if you misjudge the current direction in the gate. Sometimes a gate will be set with the gate line perpendicular to the direction in which the river in general is moving, yet the water directly between the poles may be moving at ninety degrees to the river itself (fig. 236). In this case, pointing your bow halfway between the poles and paddling straight ahead will cause you either to hit the pole toward which the current under the gate is moving or miss the gate completely. The solution is to overshoot the gate toward the side from which the perpendicular current is coming, so by the time your body passes through the gate it is centered between the poles.

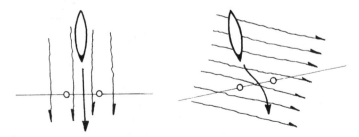

Fig. 236. *Current direction can be deceiving in otherwise simple-looking gates.* Noland Hisey

Downstream in an eddy

Not all downstream gates are set in the current. Downstreams in eddies force you to paddle across the eddy water without turning out as you would for a normal eddy turn. This requires precise edge control, stroke timing, and coordination of forward and back leans to carry forward momentum from the current through the eddy and back out into the current without losing any more speed than necessary.

To enter an eddy in which a downstream gate has been hung, start with as little crosscurrent angle as possible; your boat should be nearly parallel to the current as you cross the eddy line (fig. 237). Often the best place to enter the eddy is right next to the rock that forms it. Your last stroke in the current should be a sweep on the upstream side to continue your boat's downstream momentum and combat any upstream turning force the eddy will have on it. In a C-1 or OC-1 with your paddle on the downstream side, either holding a correction stroke as you enter the eddy or taking a powerful forward stroke will get you moving into the eddy without immediately

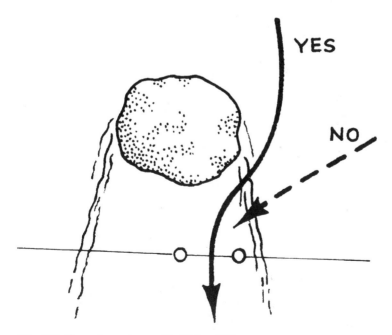

Fig. 237. *Downstream in an eddy.* Noland Hisey

eddying out. It is important in any solo canoe that you build up enough momentum before entering the eddy to carry you powerfully across the eddy line. As your boat hits the eddy water, lean into the eddy, allowing your boat to carve on the outside edge so it continues to turn downstream. When you lean into the eddy you should also lean back to prevent your bow from being affected by the eddy water as much as possible.

Once you have established your line in the eddy, lean forward and raise your stroke rate to maintain momentum. If you continue to lean back in the eddy, your boat will stall. If the next gate is tight to the downstream in the eddy, you may need to turn sharply upstream as you negotiate the downstream in the eddy. This can be done with either a reverse sweep or a duffek, using a pivot turn or a flat spin. This sharp turn will set you up for a ferry or a controlled peelout as you exit the eddy. If the next gate is well downstream of the downstream in the eddy and the current differential between the eddy and the main current is not too great, you can often simply paddle across the eddy line with your boat pointed slightly upstream of the next gate to take account of the conveyor-belt action of the river. If you leave the eddy in this way, be prepared with a downstream sweep as you cross the eddy line, since the main current will try to turn your bow downstream until you have established your line toward the next gate and your entire boat has cleared the eddy line.

Upstreams

U.S. Whitewater Team coach Bill Endicott has observed that offset downstream gates are where racers take the most penalties, while upstream gates are where they lose the most time. This is especially true of beginner racers, who often spend up to thirty seconds in an upstream gate that could be negotiated in a few seconds with the correct technique. The correct technique through upstreams allows you to smoothly convert the crosscurrent momentum you develop before entering the gate into upstream momentum to carry you through the gate and back out into the current. Another way to look at upstreams is that the shorter a line you take, the less time you will spend paddling away from the finish line. From the time you leave the current to the time you reenter it, every fraction of a second is critical.

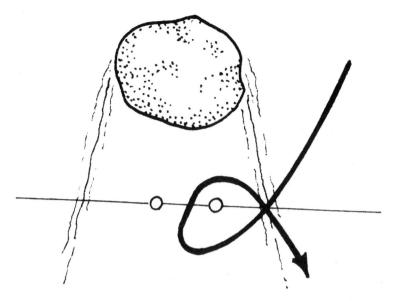

Fig. 238. *An ideal upstream.* Noland Hisey

Since there are countless variations on upstream gates, it is useful to talk about an ideal upstream as a starting point. An ideal upstream gate is set in the pocket of an eddy with a well-defined eddy line (fig. 238). The approach is from the side, allowing a paddler to develop sufficient crosscurrent drive.

To run an ideal upstream, paddle hard at the eddy, aiming your bow between the poles. Cross into the eddy with a strong forward sweep on the downstream side for kayakers and off-side canoeists. For on-side canoeists (paddle on the inside of the turn), holding a correction stroke a little longer or simply carving the outside edge slightly on the way into the gate will have a similar effect. When you initially cross the eddy line, lean your boat into the eddy. As your bow enters the gate, switch to a duffek or cross draw on the inside of the turn. This stroke should be placed as far forward as possible by reaching through the gate (fig. 239). This presumes, of course, that your entry sweep and approach have placed your bow in the gate. As you are switching to a duffek or cross draw, flatten out your lean to carve the turn on your boat's outside edge. As your boat begins to carve on its outside edge, the bow will start to rise, slowing the boat's momentum. To prevent this, lean forward slightly as you shift your side-to-side lean. Once your body has cleared the gate line, sweep on the outside of the turn and duffek downstream to exit the gate and reenter the current (figure 240).

Fig. 239. *Reaching through the gate on a cross draw.* Karen Blom

Fig. 240. *Leave an upstream as close to the gate as possible to avoid paddling up the eddy unnecessarily.* Karen Blom

Kayakers should be careful when switching from the duffek to the exit sweep not to hit the gate with their upper blade. An ideal upstream then can be done in only three strokes: entry sweep, duffek, and exit sweep. Yet the stroke sequence is the easiest part of the move to master. The subtleties of forward, back, and side-to-side leans are every bit as important and require thousands of practice runs to perfect.

C-1s will sometimes do ideal upstreams somewhat differently than the sequence described above. Because a C-1 can be pivot-turned easily, but is not as fast in a straight line as a kayak, a paddler in a C-1 will often choose to enter an ideal upstream higher than a kayaker. By sneaking his bow under the outside pole on the way in and carving his outside edge to create a dramatic pivot turn in the gate, a C-1er can get a slingshot effect to send him back into the main current. This effect is a result of the buoyancy of the boat's stern that, after being submerged in a pivot turn, squirts the boat up and forward out of the water like a pumpkin seed being shot from between your fingers. To make this kind of upstream work, you must load the duffek or cross draw by rotating your entire torso in the direction in which your boat will eventually end up heading. As the bow of the boat begins to rise, lean forward to maintain your momentum through the turn, since the risk of stalling in the gate is high.

A common mistake beginner racers make is to paddle several strokes up the eddy after clearing the gate line before peeling back into the current. At times it may be necessary to leave the eddy high in order to make the next gate, but when that is not the case, you are wasting valuable time and energy paddling even one stroke higher than necessary. To learn to leave eddies sooner, keep an eye on the inside pole. As soon as your body is past the gate line and will clear the inside pole (the pole on the inside of the turn), do your exit sweep and peel out downstream.

Less-than-ideal approach

Where the approach to an otherwise ideal upstream does not allow you to enter the eddy from across the current, you must either modify the line you take toward the eddy or do some of your turning in the current before you enter the eddy.

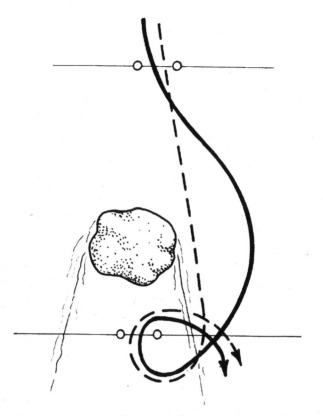

Fig. 241. *Upstream with a non-ideal approach.* Noland Hisey

If the approach is determined by the location of the gate preceding the upstream, you can often change your line simply by jogging out away from the eddy for a stroke or two before turning back toward it to drive across the current at the upstream gate (fig. 241). Although you paddle a little farther using this method, it improves your overall time on the course by allowing you to negotiate the upstream gate more quickly.

When rocks or other immovable obstacles block your cross-current approach, the solution is to take as wide a line toward the eddy as possible and start your turn into the upstream gate early. This often means sneaking your bow under the inside pole on the way in.

Upstream in the current

Upstream gates are not always set in eddies. Upstreams in the current make you paddle against the river and can be very tiring if not done correctly. Often on the first approach to such a gate you have an opportunity to get through it quickly by surfing a wave, taking advantage of a swell, or riding the boat's residual momentum through the gate. If you let this opportunity pass, however, an upstream in the current can drain your energy by requiring you to "grunt" your way up against the current.

When approaching an upstream in the current, get crosscurrent drive as you would for an ideal upstream, but turn earlier. You will usually end up sneaking your bow under the inside pole on the way into the gate. Turning early puts you into a ferry position just before entering the upstream, which is necessary because there is no eddy to help your boat turn into the gate as there is on an ideal upstream. When your bow is between the poles, your body should be as close to the gate line as possible without interfering with the ability of your inside blade to get cleanly through the gate. Leaning your boat to the outside of the turn to carve on your outside edge will also help stop your boat's downstream momentum. The slingshot effect described above for C-1 ideal upstreams can sometimes be used to move you up through the gate. If you have done everything just right up to this point, you will often be able to convert your entry duffek into a forward stroke, pulling your body through the gate, then switch quickly to an exit sweep for kayaks or off-side C-1s, or feather your duffek forward again into another duffek for on-side C-1s, and peel out downstream. Sometimes, no matter how well you approach an upstream in the current, it takes several strokes to get your body through it. In this case, be careful not to hit the poles as you paddle up through the gate, and peel out as soon as possible, keeping in mind that you only have to clear the gate by a small margin before proceeding downstream.

Merano upstream

Another way to do upstreams in the current is called a Merano upstream, after a river town in Italy where they often place upstreams in the current. Meranos work especially well when the upstream is half in the current, half in an eddy, and the approach is from directly upstream of the gate. To do a Merano,

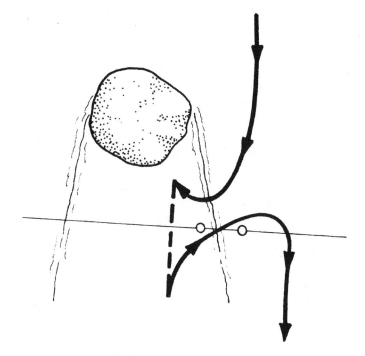

Fig. 242. *A Merano upstream.* Noland Hisey

paddle at the gate so you barely miss the pole nearest the eddy (fig. 242). The moment you pass the pole, begin a spin away from the gate. This spin can be either a flat spin or a pivot turn, depending on your boat type and the exact position of the gate. With a strong eddy, a pivot turn will give you an extra launch through the gate as the buoyancy of the stern takes over from the force of the turn; however, sometimes a flat spin is preferable, because it allows you to sideslip your boat to a position just below the gate and provides more leeway to reposition your boat at the last minute. As the spin goes past 180 degrees, you should find yourself just below the gate. Sneak your bow under the pole and use the momentum you gain from spinning in the eddy to paddle up and out of the gate. When done correctly, a Merano takes only one stroke. Deciding when a Merano is faster than a regular upstream, however, takes judgment and experience, which can be developed only by practicing and experimenting.

S turn

An s turn upstream is one that is entered from one side and exited on the opposite side (fig. 243). In general, an s turn is faster than a regular upstream, since it requires less turning, and makes it easier for a racer to conserve momentum. Of course, not all upstreams can be done as s turns, either because of the location of the gates above or below the upstream or because of the configuration of the eddy in which the upstream sits. Gates that are angled so that they are "open" to an s turn make this move even faster. For a gate to be angled this way, the inside pole should be upstream of the outside pole as shown in figure 243.

Approach an s turn eddy in the same fashion as a regular upstream. Timing of the entry sweep is also the same, but your boat and body should be closer to the inside pole than on a regular upstream. Reach your duffek or cross draw through the gate, holding it only long enough to allow your body to come even with the gate line. Now convert your duffek or cross draw into a sweep or cross sweep to begin the exit. At the same time, maintain your lean into the eddy. By not shifting your lean to

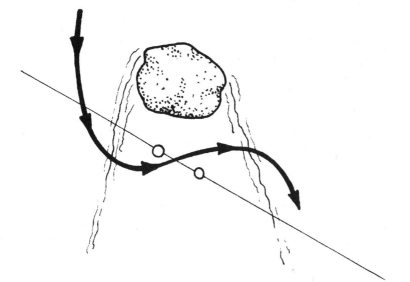

Fig. 243. *An s turn upstream. Note gate is angled to make the s turn easier.* Noland Hisey

the outside edge, you keep the boat from turning tightly upstream as it would in a regular upstream. If you have judged your boat's turning momentum correctly, the transition from duffek to sweep should smoothly change the boat's line from the first curve of the S to the second. Peel out as you normally would depending on the location of the next gate downstream.

When an s turn is placed deep in a wide midriver eddy that requires more than one stroke to get from the eddy line to the gate, you may have to enter the eddy slightly lower than you would normally to account for the eddy water's upstream movement. If you enter too high, the eddy current will pull you above the upstream before you reach the gate. You may also need to wait before doing your entry sweep, instead continuing to paddle forward until you are far enough across the eddy that the next stroke will place your boat in the gate. Leaning your boat into the eddy also helps counteract the force of the eddy water, which wants to turn you out early.

It is very important to enter the eddy high enough for an s turn, since the speed of the move depends on the turn being done in one fluid stroke that starts as a duffek and ends as a sweep. Any strokes used to paddle up the eddy to get to the gate negate the advantage of doing the upstream as an s turn. The less turning your boat can do as it executes the turn the better, since by turning less you will conserve more momentum. When done by a top racer, an s turn is one of the most graceful moves in whitewater slalom, as the boat turns slightly into the eddy, his body and paddle duck quickly through the gate, and he continues out the other side moving as fast as he was when he entered the gate.

Training for slalom

Whitewater slalom racing is a skill sport in which quick reactions on difficult whitewater moves are more important than incredible physical strength or endurance. Yet to compete at the top levels, you must be both skillful and extremely fit. Unlike some sports where repetitive, grueling workouts are the norm, in training for whitewater slalom, the more fun you're having, the more skill you're probably developing and the more fit you're becoming. Even if you don't compete seriously, training on slalom gates is a great way to stay in shape for recreational paddling.

It follows that the best training for slalom racing is paddling on whitewater gates. This helps you develop strength, endurance, and skill simultaneously, and the fitness you build is directly applicable to whitewater slalom racing. However, training on whitewater gates day in and day out breaks down even top athletes, so most racers mix whitewater gate training with flatwater distance paddling, flatwater sprints, moving-water gate training, whitewater play, and cross training in sports that emphasize hand-eye coordination such as basketball and squash, or those that use similar muscle groups such as cross-country skiing and swimming. The exact training mix each racer chooses depends on the time of year, his or her personal goals, and the availability of training sites.

To train for the U.S. team is a nearly full-time endeavor, requiring that you live close to a good whitewater river with reliable flows year-round and that you travel often to other sites to gain experience in a variety of situations. If your goals are more limited and your time or living situation is less flexible, however, you can still train effectively for local and regional competitions by taking advantage of the resources your area offers and traveling as often as possible to other rivers.

You can set up flatwater gates on almost any pond or slow-moving river where landowners will allow you to hang wires from the trees on the banks. Eight or ten gates that are adjustable in height and can be moved along their wires to make a variety of configurations will be an adequate flatwater training site. Two common types of practice gates are illustrated in figure 244 and can be constructed easily from materials available at a lumber yard. Even better than flatwater gates are moving-water gates hung on a section of river that has current and, preferably, some obstacles that form eddies, waves, and holes. Set the wires so that at least some of the gates can be hung over eddies to be used as upstreams. Angling wires so one end is farther downstream than the other can add interest to the course.

If you happen to have a whitewater river near where you live, hanging gates on a rapid will give you the best training opportunity. The best rapids for training are those that are difficult but can be climbed using the attainment techniques described earlier. Be careful to hang the gates so they are not a hazard to other boaters or a nuisance to fishermen (who can get

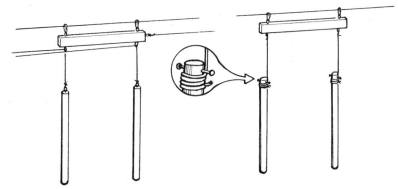

Fig. 244. *Two styles of practice gates. The type on the right is adjustable from the boat by winding more or less string onto the poles. The type on the left is only adjustable from shore.* Noland Hisey

their lines tangled in them when they cast). Monitor the course often so you can rehang or remove any downed wires—they present a danger to boaters, swimmers, and other river users.

Once you have a training site, you need to come up with a plan for your workouts. Set goals by looking ahead to races you plan to compete in and build your training schedule with an eye toward peaking at the big race or series of races. Combine endurance and strength training with pure skill training and river runs in different amounts depending on the time of year.

Since it takes longer to build endurance, emphasize it in the off-season with loop workouts on easy gates. To do a loop workout, determine a course that can be repeated several times in a continuous cycle. Paddling back up the course is done at the same intensity as paddling down the course. Loops typically take between two and sixty minutes each. Shorter loops are usually done in several sets to add up to a total "on time" of fifteen to thirty minutes. Loops longer than thirty minutes are called marathons, and one is usually enough. Another good endurance workout is flatwater distance paddling. Paddle for an hour or so at 50 percent to 70 percent of your all-out level.

As the big races approach, add more strength and speed training into the mix. Workouts where you take five runs each on five courses that are between ten and thirty seconds long are called "5-on-5s." Concentrating on such short courses gives you an opportunity to perfect a single move at full speed. Full-length courses are also good for developing speed. They help you learn to pace yourself and develop concentration in a real race situation. They should be done on whitewater if possible.

Peaking begins in the month before the big race. By reducing the number or duration of workouts and increasing their intensity, you sharpen both your physical condition and your mental psyche. Emphasizing clean runs in practice and getting plenty of rest helps you feel at the top of your form going into the big race.

Take any opportunity to be videotaped during a workout or a race. Video can be very useful in helping you visualize your paddling and gives you an objective picture of yourself. It also allows you to see improvements that may not be obvious, because they usually come about slowly rather than in quantum leaps. Any opportunity you have to be videoed during training or racing, either by a friend, coach, or interested spectator, is an opportunity to improve your skills.

Many paddlers keep training logs where they record the workouts they do each day, their race results, and often such pertinent details as diet, general health, and how they're feeling about their paddling. These can be helpful by allowing you to look back on past races and training sessions to gauge your progress over time.

WILDWATER RACING

Point-to-point racing on whitewater tests a paddler's water reading skills, reaction time, and endurance. Wildwater races usually last between ten and twenty-five minutes and are held on class II to IV whitewater. Wildwater boats are very specialized to meet the demands of the sport. They can be tippy, since they are so narrow, and they tend to be difficult to turn, because they have virtually no rocker. Wildwater open canoes often have higher gunwales than other open canoes to help them stay drier through waves.

Strategy plays an important role in wildwater racing. Whether to take advantage of the shorter line gained by cutting off a corner or let the faster water on the outside of the bend take you more quickly over a somewhat longer line is one of the many strategic decisions wildwater racers must make constant-ly as they race down the river.

Before racing on a new river, a wildwater racer may take twenty or thirty runs and scout many of the rapids from shore to familiarize himself with the lines. In each rapid, a wildwater racer will try to find the line that follows the fastest water with the least maneuvering. By tuning into subtleties such as six-inch-wide "windows" where the waves cancel each other out in the middle of seemingly channelwide wave trains, an observant wildwater racer can save the few seconds or tenths of seconds that often mean the difference between first and fifth place.

Often if a racer is unsure of a line, he will try several options, timing each one to see which is fastest. The watch is the ultimate arbiter in wildwater, so although a line may feel faster, if it is not, it should be abandoned for the line that the watch says is faster.

Wildwater racers are allowed one official practice run and one race run on a racecourse. Unlike in slalom racing, a wildwa-ter racer who swims out of his boat during the race can pull his boat to shore, hop back in, and continue without being penal-ized, although his time will certainly reflect the detour. Racers usually start at one-minute intervals, although some open-boat races use mass starts.

A wildwater racer is required to rescue other competitors who have swum out of their boats if he encounters them during his run. Even though the rescuer will certainly lose time by doing so, rescuing other racers adds an important margin of safety, since without this rule, each racer is running the river essentially alone.

Open boat

Open-boat wildwater racing takes place on class II to III water in long, narrow, high-sided canoes (fig. 245). Both double (OC-2) and single (OC-1) classes are competed.

Most open-boat tandem wildwater racers switch sides every so often in order to even out the fatigue from paddling on one side or the other. The switch is usually called by the stern paddler, who yells "hup" or something similar to alert the bow paddler. Both paddlers then take one more stroke before switch-ing. The switch itself is done by letting go of the paddle with

Fig. 245. *Open-boat wildwater racing.* Jeff Defeo

Fig. 246. *Switching technique.* Jeff Defeo

the top hand while still holding on with the bottom hand (fig. 246). The top hand then grasps the shaft, becoming the new bottom hand, while the old bottom hand lets go of the shaft but maintains contact with the thumb, which slides up the shaft until it hooks the t grip and becomes the new top hand.

Switching in the middle of a difficult rapid can be disastrous, since both paddlers are without a brace for a short time. It is best to switch in flatwater or during a lull in a rapid.

Both open-boat and closed-boat wildwater paddlers follow similar lines down rapids, looking for the fastest water, avoiding paddling through eddies where possible, staying out of waves by paddling just next to them, and trying to avoid punching holes that can significantly slow a boat. Yet open-boat wildwater paddlers must also be careful not to take on water, since it can not only slow their boat but also reduce their maneuverability.

The stroke used in wildwater is slightly different than the one described earlier under the canoe forward stroke. The wildwater stroke is fast and short, with stroke rate being more important than stroke length, so you are constantly accelerating the boat. Planting the blade in the downstream face of each wave also helps by allowing the paddle to grip the water better than when it is planted on the upstream face of a wave.

Closed boat

Decked boaters can race on more difficult whitewater than open boaters because they do not need to worry about taking on water. Maneuvering a wildwater boat down a technical class IV river is a real challenge, since a small mistake in line is compounded by the boat's lack of maneuverability.

Wildwater C-1ers and C-2ers use a stroke similar to the one described above for open canoers (fig. 247). Many C-2 wildwater paddlers also switch as open boaters do.

In kayak, the paddles now used by top wildwater racers are extremely specialized. These "wing" paddles were originally developed for flatwater kayak racing but have been adapted to wildwater (fig. 248). Their strange shape makes them a bit difficult to handle, since they cannot be feathered, but the time gained by using them is worth the trouble. The forward stroke technique necessary for using a wing paddle is more like flatwater technique than that described earlier under the kayak forward stroke. The shaft is held more horizontally during the stroke, and you swing your active arm out to the side as you pull the paddle through the water using a rhythmical swinging

Fig. 247. *Wildwater C-1 stroke technique.* Andy Bridge

Fig. 248. *A wing paddle being used in a wildwater kayak.* Andy Bridge

motion with your whole upper body. By gripping the water better, and allowing a more efficient stroke, the wing paddle has proven to be better than traditional wildwater paddles.

Training for wildwater racing

To train for either open- or closed-boat wildwater racing you need to paddle as much as possible, putting the emphasis on endurance, since competitions are mostly aerobic events. Flatwater distance is good for building endurance, but whitewater runs in a wildwater boat are even better, since they combine endurance training with skill training specific to the sport.

Because wildwater boats are so tippy, much of your early training should involve getting used to the balance of the boat. Paddling the boat on whitewater is very important, since no matter how fast you are on flatwater, if you cannot handle the most difficult rapids in a race, all is for nought.

As in training for slalom racing, it helps to have a plan. Choosing to peak for a specific race gives you something to shoot for. Keeping a training log in which you record goals, workouts, and race results can also help you quantify your improvements.

Afterword

There's much more to paddling than can be stated in writing or shown in photographs. The techniques in this book are only the physical movements of whitewater. If after reading it and practicing some of the moves you find yourself daydreaming about whitewater at school, the office, or at home, you may well have what it takes to become an addict.

Your weekends will no longer be spent working around the yard, your car will sprout funny-looking roof racks, and your garage may take on the odor of drying polypropylene long underwear. You'll travel from river to river meeting other addicts and planning your vacations around the peak runoff season. Twelve- to twenty-hour drives will become routine, but you'll wonder how you ever got along without running rivers.

Appendix A

Ensuring River Access into the Future

As the demands for electricity, outdoor recreation, open space, and developable land have increased over the last few decades, the pressure on rivers to provide these benefits has grown tremendously. Whitewater boaters, as river users, have a responsibility to the resource, other recreational users of the resource, and the public in general to make their use of the river fit in with others and with the ecology of the watershed. The politics of river running are becoming as complex as the sport itself.

In places, boaters and fishermen have a relationship not unlike the Hatfields and McCoys. Often this is due more to perceptions than realities and to the desire of each user group to have the river to themselves. These conflicts, whether real or imagined, undercut both users' credibility with resource agencies and the public. The solution in most cases is simply for each user group to respect the rights of the other for access to the river. In places, this may mean passing legislation to limit the number of paddlers on a river, or it may be as simple as establishing a voluntary agreement that boaters will try to put on after 9:30 A.M. and take off before 4:30 P.M. to give fishermen time to themselves during peak fishing hours. Whatever happens, as boaters, we need to try our best to accommodate other river users, and minimize conflicts if they arise, since our access to the river may ultimately be at stake.

Utility companies are major players on most medium to large rivers in the U.S. as are timber companies in Northern New England. In places, hydroelectric dams provide benefits to whitewater paddlers by releasing water during the summer months when the river would not normally be runnable under natural conditions. Dams also, however, often flood the best rapids and damage the local ecosystem. Nevertheless, hydro-

256

electric power is clean in the sense that it does not add greenhouse gases to the environment and its environmental impacts are mostly local, so as paddlers, we have to learn to work with utilities.

Working with utilities or corporate dam owners often means dealing with the Federal Energy Regulatory Commission, or FERC, which licenses hydropower dams in the U.S. Throughout the 1990s, hundreds of these facilities will be relicensed by FERC under a new law that requires, for the first time, that they consider recreational and environmental interests equally with hydroelectric interests on a river. This represents a once-in-a-lifetime opportunity for paddlers, anglers and others interested in rivers to influence the terms under which these companies are allowed to use the public's resource. More frequent or more regularly scheduled releases, higher minimum flows to maintain habitat, and new reservoir management practices are all likely benefits that will accrue to the environmental community as a result of this wave of relicensings.

While paddlers are often in the sport because of its individual nature, working together with other paddlers and other user groups in established clubs and coalitions is important to the continuation of free access to rivers and plentiful whitewater. This is not to say every paddler should become actively involved in resource management issues, but when a ranger or another boater asks you to move your car, wait for a minute in an eddy, or write a letter in support of a whitewater release, realize he is working to ensure that the river you enjoy paddling will still be accessible tomorrow.

The AMC is part of an environmental and recreation coalition (including the American Whitewater Affiliation, American Rivers, and others) seeking fair compensation in the form of conservation from dam owners in four major watersheds: the Androscoggin in New Hampshire and Vermont; the Deerfield in Vermont and Massachusetts; the East Branch of the Penobscot in Maine; and the Kennebec in Maine.

The owners of the dams reap the financial benefits of generating power, but they do not pay for the use of the rivers, which are a public resource. Dams can alter natural river flows, adversely effect natural habitat for fish and wildlife, and even leave some former river runs dry.

By working together, environmental and recreational users can be an equal force during relicensing proceedings, and should be able to gain improvements in river quality, flow levels, habitat and easements to protect river and reservoir shoreline. For information contact the AMC, 5 Joy Street, Boston, MA 02108.

Appendix B

Where to Learn

There are several ways to learn whitewater techniques, depending on how much money you want to spend and who you happen to know.

Learning from a friend is a great way to get into it if your friend is patient and willing to give you a thorough introduction to the sport. All too often, however, people who learn this way are either terrorized by a friend who takes them down rivers that are way over their heads or have large gaps in their knowledge, because their friend did not teach them in a systematic manner.

Many clubs offer excellent instruction programs that are taught by advanced paddlers in the club. These programs tend to be relatively well organized and systematic, although the quality of the instruction can vary considerably depending on which instructor you get. Club instruction is generally inexpensive and offers a great way to get involved in an active group of boaters from the start. See the list below for a club in your part of the country.

Clinics offered by professional outfitters tend to be more individualized than those held by clubs, but they are also significantly more expensive. The quality of the instructors is often superior to those who teach for clubs, but, although most outfitters hand out lists of active paddling clubs in the area at the end of a clinic, the link to an active group of paddlers is lacking.

The American Canoe Association certifies instructors of canoeing and kayaking at three levels: flatwater, moving water, and whitewater. The purpose of this certification is to provide a national standard of teaching competency. While not all competent teachers are ACA certified, it is a useful yardstick against which to measure a program otherwise unknown to you. Most professional schools use only ACA-certified instructors, and many club instructors are becoming certified for insurance purposes. ACA certification clinics are offered by most professional outfitters and by several clubs around the country.

Appendix C

Clubs and Outfitters

Clubs
Appalachian Mountain Club
5 Joy Street
Boston, MA 02108

Philadelphia Canoe Club
4900 Ridge Avenue
Philadelphia, PA 19128

Canoe Cruisers Association
322 10th Street SE
Washington, DC 20003

Georgia Canoeing Association
PO Box 7023
Atlanta, GA 30357

Chicago Whitewater Association
c/o Marge Cline
1343 N. Portage
Palatine, IL 60067

Keelhaulers Canoe Club
c/o Jane Allinson
375 Erieview
Sheffield Lake, OH 44054

Texas Whitewater Association
PO Drawer 5429
Austin, TX 78763

Beartooth Paddlers
PO Box 20432
Billings, MT 59104

Colorado Whitewater Association
PO Box 4315
Englewood, CO 80155–4315

River Touring Section
Sierra Club—Angeles Chapter
c/o Dave Ewoldt
9624 Saluda Avenue
Tujunga, CA 91042

Wilamette Kayak and Canoe Club
PO Box 1062
Corvallis, OR 97339

Professional Instruction Programs

Madawaska Kanu Centre
Box 635
Barry's Bay, Ontario , Canada K0J 1B0

Zoar Outdoor
PO Box 245
Charlemont, MA 01339

Nantahala Outdoor Center
41 Hwy. 19 West
Bryson City, NC 28713-9114

Otter Bar Lodge
Forks of Salmon, CA 96031

Jackson Hole Kayak School
PO Box 8695
Jackson Hole, WY 83001

Bibliography

Allan, Melinda. *Inflatable Kayak Handbook.* Boulder, CO: Johnson Books, 1991.

Bechdel, Les, and Slim Ray. *River Rescue,* second edition. Boston: AMC Books, 1989.

Davidson, J.W., and J. Rugge. *The Complete Wilderness Paddler.* New York: VIntage Books/Random, 1983.

Ford, Kent. *The Kayaker's Edge.* Durango, CO: Whitewater Instruction, 1992. Video.

———. *Solo Playboating!* Durango, CC: Whitewater Instruction, 1991. Video.

Gullion, Laurie. *Canoeing and Kayaking Instruction Manual.* Newington, VA: American Canoe Association, 1987.

Heed, Peter, and Dick Mansfield. *Canoe Racing.* Syracuse, NY: Acorn Publishing, 1992.

Hutchinson, Derek. *Eskimo Rolling.* Camden, ME: Ragged Mountain Press, 1988.

Mason, Bill. *Path of the Paddle.* Toronto: Key Porter Books, 1986.

Nealy, William. *Kayak.* Birmingham, AL: Menasha Ridge Press, 1986.

Ray, Slim. *The Canoe Handbook.* Harrisburg, PA: Stackpole Books, 1992.

Ruse, David. *Canoe Games.* London: A & C Black, 1986.

Snyder, James E. *The Squirt Book.* Birmingham, AL: Menasha Ridge Press, 1987.

U'ren, Steve. *Performance Kayaking.* Harrisburg, PA: Stackpole Books, 1990.

Walbridge, Charlie. *The Boatbuilder's Manual.* Penllyn, PA: Wildwater Designs, 1979.

About the Author

BRUCE LESSELS began paddling whitewater with the Appalachian Mountain Club at the age of 15. He has been a whitewater raft guide, a member of the U.S. Whitewater Team from 1984 to 1988, and a canoe and kayak instructor. He has paddled rivers in thirteen different countries. In 1987 he won an individual bronze medal and a team gold medal in C-1 (single closed canoe) at the Whitewater World Championships in Bourg St-Maurice, France. He founded an outdoor center on western Massachusetts' Deerfield River in 1989. His company, Zoar Outdoor, teaches whitewater canoeing and kayaking, guides whitewater raft trips, and leads sea kayaking and rock climbing trips. He has written for *Canoe* and *River Runner (Paddler)* magazines and is coauthor of the *Deerfield River Guidebook* published by New England Cartographics.

About the Appalachian Mountain Club

The Appalachian Mountain Club pursues a vigorous conservation agenda while encouraging responsible recreation, based on the philosophy that successful, long-term conservation depends upon firsthand experience of the natural environment. Fifty-seven thousand members have joined the AMC to pursue their interests in hiking, canoeing, skiing, walking, rock climbing, bicycling, camping, kayaking, and backpacking, and—at the same time—to help safeguard the environment in which these activities are possible.

Since it was founded in 1876, the Club has been at the forefront of the environmental protection movement. By cofounding several of New England's leading environmental organizations and working in coalition with these and many more groups, the AMC has positively influenced legislation and public opinion.

Volunteers in each chapter lead hundreds of outdoor activities and excursions and offer introductory instruction in backcountry sports. The AMC Education Department offers members and the public a wide range of workshops, from introductory camping to the intensive Mountain Leadership School taught on the trails of the White Mountains.

The most recent efforts in the AMC Conservation Program include river protection, Northern Forest Lands policy, Sterling Forest (NY) preservation, and support for the Clean Air Act.

The AMC's Research Department focuses on the forces affecting the ecosystem, including ozone levels, acid rain and fog, climate change, rare flora and habitat protection, and air quality and visibility.

AMC Trails

The AMC Trails Program maintains over 1,400 miles of trail (including 350 miles of the Appalachian Trail) and more than 50 shelters in the Northeast. Through a coordinated effort of volunteers, seasonal crews, and program staff, the AMC contributes more than 10,000 hours of public service work each summer in the area from Washington, DC to Maine.

In addition to supporting our work by becoming an AMC member, hikers can donate time as volunteers. The Club offers four unique weekly volunteer base camps in New Hampshire, Maine, Massachusetts, and New York. We also sponsor ten-day service projects throughout the United States, Adopt-a-Trail programs, trails day events, trail skills workshops, and chapter and camp volunteer projects.

The AMC has a longstanding connection to Acadia National Park. Working in cooperation with the National Park Service and Friends of Acadia, the AMC Trails Program provides many opportunities to preserve the park's resources. These include half-day volunteer projects for guests at AMC's Echo Lake Camp, ten-day service projects, week-long volunteer crews in the fall, and trails day events. For more information on these public service volunteer opportunities, contact the AMC Trails Program, Pinkham Notch Visitor Center, P.O. Box 298, Gorham, NH 03581; 603-466-2721.

The Club operates eight alpine huts in the White Mountains that provide shelter, bunks and blankets, and hearty meals for hikers. Pinkham Notch Visitor Center, at the foot of Mt. Washington, is base camp to the adventurous and the ideal location for individuals and families new to outdoor recreation. Comfortable bunkrooms, mountain hospitality, and home-cooked, family-style meals make Pinkham Notch Visitor Center a fun and affordable choice for lodging. For reservations, call 603-466-2727.

At the AMC headquarters in Boston and at Pinkham Notch Visitor Center in New Hampshire, the bookstore and information center stock the entire line of AMC publications, as well as other trail and river guides, maps, reference materials, and the latest articles on conservation issues. Guidebooks and other AMC gifts are available by mail order (AMC, P.O. Box 298, Gorham, NH 03581), or call toll-free 800-262-4455. Also available from the bookstore or by subscription is *Appalachia*, the country's oldest mountaineering and conservation journal.

Index